LANDMARK DECISIONS OF THE UNITED STATES SUPREME COURT III

MAUREEN HARRISON & STEVE GILBERT
EDITORS

LANDMARK DECISIONS SERIES

EXCELLENT BOOKS
BEVERLY HILLS, CALIFORNIA

EXCELLENT BOOKS
Post Office Box 7121
Beverly Hills, CA 90212-7121

"This publication is designed to provide accurate and authoritative information in regard to the subject matter covered. It is sold with the understanding that the publisher is not engaged in rendering legal or other professional service. If legal advice or other expert assistance is required, the services of a competent professional person should be sought." - From a Declaration of Principles jointly adopted by a Committee of the American Bar Association and a Committee of Publishers.

Publisher's Cataloging in Publication Data

Landmark Decisions Of The United States Supreme Court III/
Maureen Harrison, Steve Gilbert, editors.
 p. cm. - (Landmark Decisions Series)
Bibliography: p.
Includes Index.
1. United States. Supreme Court.
I. Title. II. Harrison, Maureen. III. Gilbert, Steve.
IV. Series: Landmark Decisions.
KF8742.H24 1991   LC 90-84578
347.'73'26-dc20
[347.30726]
ISBN 0-9628014-3-7
ISBN 0-9628014-0-2 (Landmark Decisions Series)

A Note To The Reader

Chiseled into the facade of the United States Supreme Court Building are these words:

EQUAL JUSTICE UNDER THE LAW

For many Americans, famous, infamous, and ordinary, the U.S. Supreme Court has been the last stop in their personal search for that elusive "equal justice under the law." This book is about some of those Americans: two Presidents, a draft protester, a mentally ill woman, seven black teenagers, three schoolchildren, an imprisoned woman, a white man and his black wife, two school teachers, a female office worker and her male supervisor, two religious groups and their holiday symbols. People with little or nothing in common except that their personal search for equal justice led them one by one to the U.S. Supreme Court.

The Court has the final word on all Constitutional questions arising in the Federal Courts and all Federal questions arising in the State Courts. Since 1791 the Supreme Court has issued thousands of individual decisions. All have been important to the parties involved, but some, a significant few, have grown so important as to involve all Americans. These are Landmark Decisions, fundamentally altering the relationships of Americans to their institutions and to each other. Of these significant few, we have selected twelve for inclusion in this book. These decisions, issued over the span of 186 years, represent some of the great and continuing controversies of American history and politics. They are presented here in plain english synopsis for the first time to the general reader.

On the first Monday of each October the United States Supreme Court begins a new Term. From all over the country, on all kinds of issues, and for all kinds of reasons, Americans bring controversies to the Court for a final disposition. The Founding Fathers created the Supreme Court to construct and interpret the meaning of the Constitution. Chief Justice Charles Evans Hughes summed up the Court's responsibility in this way: "We are under a Constitution, but the Constitution is what the Judges say it is."

Every year over five thousand requests for review of lower court decisions are received by the Court. Requests, called *petitions for certiorari*, come to the Court from the losing side in Federal Appeals Courts or State Supreme Courts. Four of the nine justices must agree to a review. Review is accepted in only four hundred cases each year. Once accepted, written arguments [briefs] pro and con are submitted to the Court by both the petitioner, the side appealing the lower court decision against them, and the respondent, the side defending the lower court decision in their favor. Interested parties, called *amici curiae*, friends of the court, may be permitted to file briefs in support of either side. After the briefs are submitted to and reviewed by the Justices, public oral arguments are heard by the Court in the Supreme Court chamber. Ordinarily the opposing sides, petitioner and respondent, are given thirty minutes of oral argument. (In *U.S. v. Nixon* oral arguments lasted an extraordinary three hours.) The Justices, at their discretion, may interrupt at any time to require further explanations, to pose hypothetical questions, or make observations. Twice a week, on Wednesday and Friday, the Justices meet alone in conference to discuss each case and vote on its outcome. They may affirm [let stand] or reverse [change the outcome of], in whole or in part, the decisions of the lower courts from which these appeals have come. One

Justice, voting in the majority, will be selected to write the majority opinion. Others may join in the majority opinion, write their own concurring opinion, write their own dissenting opinion, or join in another's concurrence or dissent. Drafts of the majority, concurring, and dissenting opinions circulate among the Justices, are redrafted and recirculated, until a consensus is reached and a decision announced. It is the majority opinion as finally issued by the Court that stands as the law of the land. All other Courts, Federal and State, are bound by Supreme Court precedent.

Judge Learned Hand wrote: "The language of the law must not be foreign to the ears of those who are to obey it." The twelve Landmark Decisions presented in this book are carefully edited versions of the official texts issued by the Supreme Court in *United States Reports.* We, as editors, have made every effort to replace esoteric legalese with plain english without damaging the original decisions. Edited out are long alpha-numeric legal citations and wordy wrangles over points of procedure. Edited in are definitions (*writ of habeas corpus* = an order from a judge to bring a person to court), translations (*certiorari* = the decision of the Court to review a case), identifications (Appellant = William Marbury, Appellee = James Madison), and explanations (where the case originated, how it got to the court, and who the parties were).

You will find in this book the majority opinion of the Court as expressed by the Justice chosen to speak for the Court. Preceding each edited decision, we note where the complete decision can be found. The bibliography provides a list of further reading on the cases and the Court. Also included for the reader's reference is a complete copy of the U.S. Constitution, to which every decision refers.

This is the third book in the **Landmark Decisions Series.** In each we have attempted to give you an equal mix of history, controversy, and politics.

Landmark Decisions I presented cases on School Desegregation, Obscenity, School Prayer, Fair Trials, Sexual Privacy, Censorship, Abortion, Affirmative Action, Book Banning, and Flag Burning.

Landmark Decisions II presented cases on Slavery, Women's Suffrage, Japanese American Concentration Camps, Bible Reading In The Public Schools, A Book Banned In Boston, The Rights of the Accused, The Death Penalty, Homosexuality, Offensive Speech, and the Right To Die.

Landmark Decisions III deals with Court rulings on Executive Privilege, Limits of Free Speech, Forced Sterilization, Mob Justice, The Pledge of Allegiance, Illegal Search and Seizure, Interracial Marriage, Monkey Trials, Sexual Harassment in the Workplace, and Separation of Church and State.

In all of our books we have strived to bring the words of the Justices from the courthouse into your house. Chief Justice John Marshall said the Court's decision "comes home in its effects to every man's fireside; it passes on his property, his reputation, his life, his all." We entered into editing this series because we, like you, and your family and friends, must obey, under penalty of law, the decisions of the U.S. Supreme Court. It stands to reason that, if we owe them our obedience, then we owe it to ourselves to know what they say, not second-hand, but for ourselves. We think it's time for you to have the final word.

M.H. & S.G.

This book is dedicated to our son,

Scott

ABOUT THE EDITORS

MAUREEN HARRISON is a textbook editor and a
member of the Supreme Court Historical Society

STEVE GILBERT is a law librarian and a member of the
American Association of Law Libraries and the American
Bar Association

TABLE OF CONTENTS

"It is emphatically the province and duty of the judicial department to say what the law is. . . . The judicial power of the United States is extended to all cases arising under the constitution."
Chief Justice John Marshall
Marbury v. Madison (1803)

"[W]e conclude that the legitimate needs of the judicial process may outweigh Presidential privilege."
Chief Justice Warren Burger
United States v. Nixon (1974)

"The most stringent protection of free speech would not protect a man falsely shouting fire in a theater, and causing a panic. . . ."
Justice Oliver Wendell Holmes
Schenck v. United States (1919)

"It is better for all the world, if instead of waiting to execute degenerate offspring for crime, or to let them starve for their imbecility, society can prevent those who are manifestly unfit from continuing their kind. . . . Three generations of imbeciles are enough."
Justice Oliver Wendell Holmes
Buck v. Bell (1927)

MOB JUSTICE
53

"[A] defendant, charged with a serious crime, must not be stripped of his right to have sufficient time to advise with counsel and prepare his defense. To do that is . . . to go forward with the haste of the mob."
Justice George Sutherland
Scottsboro Boys v. Alabama (1932)

PLEDGE OF ALLEGIANCE
69

"'[T]he flag is the symbol of the Nation's power, the emblem of freedom in its truest, best sense . . . it signifies government resting on the consent of the governed. . . .'"
Justice Felix Frankfurter
Minersville School District v. Gobitis (1940)

"To believe that patriotism will not flourish if patriotic ceremonies are voluntary and spontaneous instead of a compulsory routine is to make an unflattering estimate of the appeal of our institutions to free minds."
Justice Robert Jackson
Board of Education v. Barnette (1943)

ILLEGAL SEARCH & SEIZURE
97

"Nothing can destroy a government more quickly than its failure to observe its own laws, or worse, its disregard of the charter of its own existence."
Justice Thomas Clark
Mapp v. Ohio (1961)

INTERRACIAL MARRIAGE
113

"The freedom to marry has long been recognized as one of the vital personal rights essential to the orderly pursuit of happiness by free men."
Chief Justice Earl Warren
Loving v. Virginia (1967)

MONKEY TRIALS
125

"Government in our democracy, state and national, must be neutral in matters of religious theory, doctrine, and practice. It may not be hostile to any religion or to the advocacy of no-religion; and it may not aid, foster, or promote one religion or religious theory against another or even against the militant opposite."
Justice Abe Fortas
Epperson v. Arkansas (1968)

"As the law thus stands, while the theory of evolution of man may not be taught in the schools of the state, nothing contrary to that theory is required to be taught."
Tennessee Chief Justice Grafton Green
Scopes v. Tennessee (1927)

SEXUAL HARASSMENT
151

"'Sexual harassment which creates a hostile or offensive environment for members of one sex is every bit the arbitrary barrier to sexual equality at the workplace that racial harassment is to racial equality.'"
Justice William Rehnquist
Meritor Savings Bank v. Vinson (1986)

CHURCH & STATE
169
"A secular state, it must be remembered, is not the same as an atheistic or antireligious state. A secular state establishes neither atheism nor religion as its official creed."
Justice Harry Blackmun
Allegheny County v. ACLU (1989)

THE U.S. CONSTITUTION
195
"We the people of the United States, in order to form a more perfect union, establish justice, insure domestic tranquility, provide for the common defense, promote the general welfare, and secure the blessings of liberty to ourselves and our posterity, do ordain and establish this Constitution for the United States of America."
The Preamble (1789)

EXECUTIVE PRIVILEGE

MARBURY v. MADISON

In the Election of 1800 President John Adams, the Federalist Party candidate, was defeated for re-election by the Democrat Republican Party candidate, Thomas Jefferson. Jefferson was to take the oath of office on March 4, 1801. On February 27 the Federalist-dominated Congress passed an Act allowing President Adams to appoint 42 Justices of the Peace for the District of Columbia. On March 2 the President nominated 42 of his Federalist supporters. The lame duck Senate advised and consented to the appointments on March 3. To hold their offices as Justices of the Peace the appointees required signed and sealed Commissions. President Adams signed the Commissions and the Great Seal of the United States was placed upon them. In the last hours of the Adams Administration the Acting Secretary of State, John Marshall, failed to deliver the Commissions to the appointees. Marshall later wrote: "I should . . . have sent out the commissions which had been signed and sealed but for the the extreme hurry of the time."

On March 4, 1801 Thomas Jefferson became President of the United States. John Marshall, who as Adams' Secretary of State had failed to deliver the commissions, became the Chief Justice of the Supreme Court. Jefferson, based on their failure to possess the signed and sealed commissions, which he would not deliver to them, refused to recognize the validity of the appointment of the "mid-night judges." In December 1801 William Marbury, one of the 42 disappointed appointees, petitioned the Court to compel Jefferson's Secretary of State, James Madison, to deliver his commission.

The decision of the Supreme Court was announced on February 24, 1803 by Chief Justice John Marshall.

The complete text of *Marbury v. Madison* appears in volume 5 of *United States Reports.*

MARBURY v. MADISON

FEBRUARY 24, 1803

CHIEF JUSTICE JOHN MARSHALL delivered the opinion of the Court: At the last term, . . . a rule was granted in this case, requiring the secretary of state [James Madison] to show cause why a *mandamus* [court order] should not issue, directing him to deliver to William Marbury his commission as a justice of the peace for the county of Washington, in the district of Columbia.

No cause has been shown, and the present motion [request to the court] is for a [court order]. The peculiar delicacy of this case, the novelty of some of its circumstances, and the real difficulty attending the points which occur in it, require a complete exposition of the principles on which the opinion to be given by the court is founded.

. . . . In the order in which the court has viewed this subject, the following questions have been considered and decided.

First. Has the applicant a right to the commission he demands?

. . . . His right originates in an act of congress passed in February, 1801, concerning [appointment of Justices of the Peace in] the district of Columbia.

. . . . It appears, from the affidavits, that in compliance with this law, a commission for William Marbury, as a justice of peace for the county of Washington, was signed by John Adams, then President of the United States; after which the seal of the United States was affixed to it; but the commission has never reached the person for whom it was made out.

. . . . It is . . . decidedly the opinion of the court, that when a commission has been signed by the president, the appointment is made; and that the commission is complete when the seal of the United States has been affixed to it by the secretary of state.

. . . . Mr. Marbury, then, since his commission was signed by the president, and sealed by the secretary of state, was appointed; and as the law creating the office, gave the officer a right to hold for five years, independent of the executive, the appointment was not revocable, but vested in the officer legal rights, which are protected by the laws of his country.

To withhold his commission, therefore, is an act deemed by the court not warranted by law, but violative of a vested legal right.

. . . . Secondly. If he has a right, and that right has been violated, do the laws of his country afford him a remedy?

The very essence of civil liberty certainly consists in the right of every individual to claim the protection of the laws, whenever he receives an injury. One of the first duties of government is to afford that protection. In Great Britain the king himself is sued in the respectful form of a petition, and he never fails to comply with the judgment of his court.

. . . . The government of the United States has been emphatically termed a government of laws, and not of men. It will certainly cease to deserve this high appellation, if the laws furnish no remedy for the violation of a vested legal right.

. . . . By the constitution of the United States, the president is invested with certain important political powers, in the exercise of which he is to use his own discretion, and is accountable only to his country in his political character and to his own conscience. To aid him in the performance of these duties, he is authorized to appoint certain officers, who act by his authority, and in conformity with his orders.

. . . . The power of nominating to the senate, and the power of appointing the person nominated, are political powers, to be exercised by the president according to his own discretion. When he has made an appointment, he has exercised his whole power, and his discretion has been completely applied to the case. If, by law, the officer be removable at the will of the president, then a new appointment may be immediately made, and the rights of the officer are terminated. But as a fact which has existed cannot be made never to have existed, the appointment cannot be annihilated; and, consequently, if the officer is by law not removable at the will of the president, the rights he has acquired are protected by the law, and are not resumable by the president. They cannot be extinguished by executive authority. . . .

It is, then, the opinion of the court,

First. That by signing the commission of Mr. Marbury, the President of the United States appointed him a justice of peace for the county of Washington, in the district of Columbia; and that the seal of the United States, affixed thereto by the secretary of state, is conclusive testimony of the verity of the signature, and of the completion of the appointment; and that the appointment conferred on him a legal right to the office for the space of five years.

Secondly. That, having this legal title to the office, he has a consequent right to the commission; a refusal to deliver which is a plain violation of that right, for which the laws of his country afford him a remedy.

. . . . Thirdly. He is entitled to the remedy for which he applies. . . .

The act to establish the judicial courts of the United States authorizes the supreme court "to issue [court orders], in cases warranted by the principles and usages of law, to any courts appointed, or persons holding office, under the authority of the United States."

The secretary of state, being a person holding an office under the authority of the United States, is precisely within the letter of the description; and if this court is not authorized to issue [an order] to such an officer, it must be because the law is unconstitutional, and therefore absolutely incapable of conferring the authority, and assigning the duties which its words purport to confer and assign.

The constitution vests the whole judicial power of the United States in one supreme court. . . . This power is expressly extended to all cases arising under the laws of the United States; and, consequently, in some form, may be exercised over the present case; because the right claimed is given by a law of the United States.

In the distribution of this power it is declared that "the supreme court shall have original jurisdiction in all cases affecting ambassadors, other public ministers and consuls, and those in which a state shall be a party. In all other cases, the supreme court shall have appellate jurisdiction."

. . . . The question, whether an act, repugnant to the constitution, can become the law of the land, is a question deeply interesting to the United States; but, happily, not of an intricacy proportioned to its interest. It seems only necessary to recognise certain principles, supposed to have been long and well established, to decide it.

That the people have an original right to establish, for their future government, such principles as, in their opinion, shall most conduce to their own happiness is the basis on which the whole American fabric has been erected. The exercise of this original right is a very great exertion; nor can it, nor ought it, to be frequently repeated. The principles, therefore, so established, are deemed fundamental. And as the authority from which they proceed is supreme, and can seldom act, they are designed to be permanent.

This original and supreme will organizes the government, and assigns to different departments their respective powers. It may either stop here, or establish certain limits not to be transcended by those departments.

The government of the United States is of the latter description. The powers of the legislature are defined and limited; and that those limits may not be mistaken, or forgotten, the constitution is written. To what purpose are powers limited, and to what purpose is that limitation committed to writing, if these limits may, at any time, be passed by those intended to be restrained? The distinction between a government with limited and unlimited powers is abolished, if those limits do not confine the persons on whom they are imposed, and if acts prohibited and acts allowed, are of equal obligation. It is a proposition too plain to be contested, that the constitution controls any legislative act repugnant to it; or, that the legislature may alter the constitution by an ordinary act.

Between these alternatives there is no middle ground. The constitution is either a superior paramount law, unchangeable by ordinary means, or it is on a level with ordinary legislative acts, and, like other acts, is alterable when the legislature shall please to alter it.

If the former part of the alternative be true, then a legislative act contrary to the constitution is not law: if the latter part be true, then written constitutions are absurd attempts, on the part of the people, to limit a power in its own nature illimitable.

Certainly all those who have framed written constitutions contemplate them as forming the fundamental and paramount law of the nation, and, consequently, the theory of every such government must be, that an act of the legislature, repugnant to the constitution, is void.

This theory is essentially attached to a written constitution, and, is consequently, to be considered, by this court, as one of the fundamental principles of our society. It is not therefore to be lost sight of in the further consideration of this subject.

If an act of the legislature, repugnant to the constitution, is void, does it, notwithstanding its invalidity, bind the courts, and oblige them to give it effect? Or, in other words, though it be not law, does it constitute a rule as operative as if it was a law? This would be to overthrow in fact what was established in theory; and would seem, at first view, an absurdity too gross to be insisted on. It shall, however, receive a more attentive consideration.

It is emphatically the province and duty of the judicial department to say what the law is. Those who apply the rule to particular cases, must of necessity expound and interpret that rule. If two laws conflict with each other, the courts must decide on the operation of each.

So if a law be in opposition to the constitution; if both the law and the constitution apply to a particular case, so that the court must either decide that case conformably to the law, disregarding the constitution; or conformably to the constitution, disregarding the law; the court must determine which of these conflicting rules governs the case. This is of the very essence of judicial duty.

If, then, the courts are to regard the constitution, and the constitution is superior to any ordinary act of the legislature, the constitution, and not such ordinary act, must govern the case to which they both apply.

Those, then, who controvert the principle that the constitution is to be considered, in court, as a paramount law, are reduced to the necessity of maintaining that courts must close their eyes on the constitution, and see only the law.

This doctrine would subvert the very foundation of all written constitutions. It would declare that an act which, according to the principles and theory of our government, is entirely void, is yet, in practice, completely obligatory. It would declare that if the legislature shall do what is expressly forbidden, such act, notwithstanding the express prohibition, is in reality effectual. It would be giving to the legislature a practical and real omnipotence, with the same breath which professes to restrict their powers within narrow limits. It is prescribing limits, and declaring that those limits may be passed at pleasure.

That it thus reduces to nothing what we have deemed the greatest improvement on political institutions, a written constitution, would of itself be sufficient, in America, where written constitutions have been viewed with so much reverence, for rejecting the construction. But the peculiar expressions of the constitution of the United States furnish additional arguments in favour of its rejection.

The judicial power of the United States is extended to all cases arising under the constitution.

Could it be the intention of those who gave this power, to say that in using it the constitution should not be looked into? That a case arising under the constitution should be decided without examining the instrument under which it arises?

This is too extravagant to be maintained.

In some cases, then, the constitution must be looked into by the judges. And if they can open it at all, what part of it are they forbidden to read or to obey?

. . . . [I]t is apparent, that the framers of the constitution contemplated that instrument as a rule for the government of *courts*, as well as of the legislature.

Why otherwise does it direct the judges to take an oath to support it? This oath certainly applies in an especial manner, to their conduct in their official character. How immoral to impose it on them, if they were to be used as the instruments, and the knowing instruments, for violating what they swear to support!

The oath of office, too, imposed by the legislature, is completely demonstrative of the legislative opinion on this subject. It is in these words: "I do solemnly swear that I will administer justice without respect to persons, and do equal right to the poor and to the rich; and that I will faithfully and impartially discharge all the duties incumbent on me as _____ , according to the best of my abilities and understanding, agreeably to *the constitution* and laws of the United States."

Why does a judge swear to discharge his duties agreeably to the constitution of the United States, if that constitution forms no rule for his government? if it is closed upon him, and cannot be inspected by him?

If such be the real state of things, this is worse than solemn mockery. To prescribe, or to take this oath, becomes equally a crime.

It is also not entirely unworthy of observation, that in declaring what shall be the *supreme* law of the land, the *constitution* itself is first mentioned; and not the laws of the United States generally, but those only which shall be made in *pursuance* of the constitution, have that rank.

Thus, the particular phraseology of the constitution of the
United States confirms and strengthens the principle,
supposed to be essential to all written constitutions, that a
law repugnant to the constitution is void; and that *courts*,
as well as other departments, are bound by that
instrument.

The rul[ing in favor of Marbury] must be [obeyed].

EXECUTIVE PRIVILEGE

UNITED STATES v. NIXON

On February 25, 1974 a Grand Jury in Washington, D.C. investigating the Watergate cover-up indicted seven individuals - know as the "White House Plumbers" - on charges of conspiracy and obstruction of justice. Richard Nixon, President of the United States, was named by the Grand Jury as an unindicted co-conspirator.

The Government's Special Prosecutor, Leon Jaworski, requested that U.S. District Court Judge John Sirica issue a subpoena to President Nixon demanding he surrender to the Court, before the trial of the seven defendants, certain White House tapes and papers relating to conversations between the President and his aides and advisors.

The President's counsel argued against the issuance of the subpoena on the grounds that the President's communications were protected by executive privilege - an absolute right of presidential privacy preventing any Court, under the separation of powers provision of the Constitution, from access to presidential papers or tapes.

The District Court rejected the President's claim on May 4. Judge Sirica held that the Courts, not the President, would determine what was, and what was not, privileged. The Court issued a subpoena and the President appealed.

On May 31, 1974, at the request of the President and the Special Prosecutor, the United States Supreme Court accepted the case for review.

Oral arguments were heard before the Court on July 8, 1974 and a decision was announced on July 24, 1974 by Chief Justice Warren Burger.

The complete text of *United States v. Nixon* can be found in volume 418 of *United States Reports.*

UNITED STATES v. NIXON

JULY 24, 1974

CHIEF JUSTICE WARREN BURGER delivered the opinion of the Court: This litigation presents for review the denial of a motion [request to the court] . . . to quash [annul] a . . . subpoena [demand for materials] . . . issued by the United States District Court for the District of Columbia, . . . direct[ing] the President to produce certain tape recordings and documents relating to his conversations with aides and advisers. The [District] court rejected the President's claims of absolute executive privilege. . . . The President [and Special Prosecutor] appealed [and we agreed to hear the case] because of the public importance of the issues presented and the need for their prompt resolution.

On March 1, 1974, a grand jury of the United States District Court for the District of Columbia returned an indictment charging seven named individuals [John N. Mitchell, H.R. Haldeman, John D. Ehrlichman, Charles W. Colson, Robert C. Mardian, Kenneth W. Parkinson, and Gordon Strachan] with various offenses, including conspiracy to defraud the United States and to obstruct justice. Although he was not designated as such in the indictment, the grand jury named the President, among others, as an unindicted co-conspirator. On April 18, 1974, upon motion of the Special Prosecutor, a subpoena . . . was issued . . . to the President by the United States District Court and made returnable [to the court] on May 2, 1974. This subpoena required the production, in advance of the September 9 trial date, of certain tapes, memoranda, papers, transcripts, or other writings relating

to certain precisely identified meetings between the
President and others. The Special Prosecutor was able to
fix the time, place, and persons present at these
discussions because the White House daily logs and
appointment records had been delivered to him. On April
30, the President publicly released edited transcripts of 43
conversations; portions of 20 conversations subject to
subpoena in the present case were included. On May 1,
1974, the President's counsel filed a . . . motion to quash
the subpoena. . . .

On May 20, 1974, the District Court denied the
motion. . . . It further ordered "the President or any
subordinate officer, official, or employee with custody or
control of the documents or objects subpoenaed," to
deliver to the District Court, on or before May 31, 1974,
the originals of all subpoenaed items, as well as an index
and analysis of those items, together with tape copies of
those portions of the subpoenaed recordings for which
transcripts had been released to the public by the
President on April 30. . . .

The District Court held that the judiciary, not the
President, was the final arbiter of a claim of executive
privilege.   The court concluded that, under the
circumstances of this case, the [executive] privilege was
overcome by the Special Prosecutor's . . . "demonstration
of need sufficiently compelling to warrant judicial
examination in chambers. . . ." The court . . . provided
that matters filed under seal [kept confidential] remain
under seal when transmitted as part of the record. . . .

[W]e turn to the claim that the subpoena should be
quashed because it demands "confidential conversations
between a President and his close advisors that it would

be inconsistent with the public interest to produce." The first contention is a broad claim that the separation of powers doctrine precludes judicial review of a President's claim of privilege. The second contention is that if he does not prevail on the claim of absolute privilege, the court should hold as a matter of constitutional law that the privilege prevails over the subpoena. . . .

In the performance of assigned constitutional duties each branch of the Government must initially interpret the Constitution, and the interpretation of its powers by any branch is due great respect from the others. The President's counsel, as we have noted, reads the Constitution as providing an absolute privilege of confidentiality for all Presidential communications. Many decisions of this Court, however, have unequivocally reaffirmed the holding of *Marbury v. Madison* that "[i]t is emphatically the province and duty of the judicial department to say what the law is."

No holding of the Court has defined the scope of judicial power specifically relating to the enforcement of a subpoena for confidential Presidential communications for use in a criminal prosecution, but other exercises of power by the Executive Branch and the Legislative Branch have been found invalid as in conflict with the Constitution. . . . Since this Court has consistently exercised the power to construe and delineate claims arising under express powers, it must follow that the Court has authority to interpret claims with respect to powers alleged to derive from enumerated powers.

Our system of government "requires that federal courts on occasion interpret the Constitution in a manner at variance with the construction given the document by another branch." And in *Baker v. Carr*, the Court stated:

"Deciding whether a matter has in any measure been committed by the Constitution to another branch of government, or whether the action of that branch exceeds whatever authority has been committed, is itself a delicate exercise in constitutional interpretation, and is a responsibility of this Court as ultimate interpreter of the Constitution."

Notwithstanding the deference each branch must accord the others, the "judicial Power of the United States" vested in the federal courts by Art. III, Section 1, of the Constitution can no more be shared with the Executive Branch than the Chief Executive, for example, can share with the Judiciary the veto power, or the Congress share with the Judiciary the power to override a Presidential veto. Any other conclusion would be contrary to the basic concept of separation of powers and the checks and balances that flow from the scheme of a tripartite government. We therefore reaffirm that it is the province and duty of this Court "to say what the law is" with respect to the claim of privilege presented in this case.

In support of his claim of absolute privilege, the President's counsel urges two grounds, one of which is common to all governments and one of which is peculiar to our system of separation of powers. The first ground is the valid need for protection of communications between high Government officials and those who advise and assist them in the performance of their manifold duties; the importance of this confidentiality is too plain

to require further discussion. Human experience teaches
that those who expect public dissemination of their
remarks may well temper candor with a concern for
appearances and for their own interests to the detriment
of the decisionmaking process. Whatever the nature of
the privilege of confidentiality of Presidential
communications in the exercise of Art. II powers, the
privilege can be said to derive from the supremacy of
each branch within its own assigned area of constitutional
duties. Certain powers and privileges flow from the
nature of enumerated powers; the protection of the
confidentiality of Presidential communications has similar
constitutional underpinnings.

The second ground asserted by the President's counsel in
support of the claim of absolute privilege rests on the
doctrine of separation of powers. Here it is argued that
the independence of the Executive Branch within its own
sphere insulates a President from a judicial subpoena in
an ongoing criminal prosecution, and thereby protects
confidential Presidential communications.

However, neither the doctrine of separation of powers,
nor the need for confidentiality of high-level
communications, without more, can sustain an absolute,
unqualified Presidential privilege of immunity from
judicial process under all circumstances. The President's
need for complete candor and objectivity from advisers
calls for great deference from the courts. However, when
the privilege depends solely on the broad,
undifferentiated claim of public interest in the
confidentiality of such conversations, a confrontation with
other values arises. [Without] a claim of need to protect
military, diplomatic, or sensitive national security secrets,
we find it difficult to accept the argument that even the

very important interest in confidentiality of Presidential communications is significantly diminished by production of such material for *in camera* [private] inspection with all the protection that a district court will be obliged to provide.

The impediment that an absolute, unqualified privilege would place in the way of the primary constitutional duty of the Judicial Branch to do justice in criminal prosecutions would plainly conflict with the function of the courts under Art. III. In designing the structure of our Government and dividing and allocating the sovereign power among three co-equal branches, the Framers of the Constitution sought to provide a comprehensive system, but the separate powers were not intended to operate with absolute independence.

. . . . To read the Art. II powers of the President as providing an absolute privilege as against a subpoena essential to enforcement of criminal statutes on no more than a generalized claim of the public interest in confidentiality of nonmilitary and nondiplomatic discussions would upset the constitutional balance of "a workable government" and gravely impair the role of the courts under Art. III.

Since we conclude that the legitimate needs of the judicial process may outweigh Presidential privilege, it is necessary to resolve those competing interests in a manner that preserves the essential functions of each branch. The right and indeed the duty to resolve that question does not free the Judiciary from according high respect to the representations made on behalf of the President.

The expectation of a President to the confidentiality of
his conversations and correspondence . . . has all the
values to which we accord deference for the privacy of all
citizens and, added to those values, is the necessity for
protection of the public interest in candid, objective, and
even blunt or harsh opinions in Presidential decisionmaking. A President and those who assist him must be
free to explore alternatives in the process of shaping
policies and making decisions and to do so in a way many
would be unwilling to express except privately. These are
the considerations justifying a presumptive privilege for
Presidential communications. The privilege is
fundamental to the operation of Government and
inextricably rooted in the separation of powers under the
Constitution. In *Nixon v. Sirica*, the Court of Appeals
held that such Presidential communications are
"presumptively privileged," and this position is accepted
by both parties in [this case]. We agree with Chief Justice
Marshall's observation [in *United States v. Burr*],
therefore, that "[i]n no case of this kind would a court be
required to proceed against the president as against an
ordinary individual."

But this presumptive privilege must be considered in light
of our historic commitment to the rule of law. This is
nowhere more profoundly manifest than in our view that
"the twofold aim [of criminal justice] is that guilt shall
not escape or innocence suffer." We have elected to
employ an adversary system of criminal justice in which
the parties contest all issues before a court of law. The
need to develop all relevant facts in the adversary system
is both fundamental and comprehensive. The ends of
criminal justice would be defeated if judgments were to
be founded on a partial or speculative presentation of the
facts. The very integrity of the judicial system and public

confidence in the system depend on full disclosure of all the facts. . . . To ensure that justice is done, it is imperative to the function of courts that compulsory process be available for the production of evidence needed either by the prosecution or by the defense.

. . . . [T]he Fifth Amendment to the Constitution provides that no man "shall be compelled in any criminal case to be a witness against himself." And, generally, an attorney or a priest may not be required to disclose what has been revealed in professional confidence. These and other interests are recognized in law by privileges against forced disclosure, established in the Constitution, by statute, or at common law. Whatever their origins, these exceptions to the demand for every man's evidence are not lightly created nor expansively construed, for they are in derogation of the search for truth.

In this case the President challenges a subpoena served on him as a third party requiring the production of materials for use in a criminal prosecution; he does so on the claim that he has a privilege against disclosure of confidential communications. He does not place his claim of privilege on the ground they are military or diplomatic secrets. As to these areas of Art. II duties the courts have traditionally shown the utmost deference to Presidential responsibilities. . . .

No case of the Court, however, has extended this high degree of deference to a President's generalized interest in confidentiality. Nowhere in the Constitution, as we have noted earlier, is there any explicit reference to a privilege of confidentiality, yet to the extent this interest relates to the effective discharge of a President's powers, it is constitutionally based.

The right to the production of all evidence at a criminal trial similarly has constitutional dimensions. The Sixth Amendment explicitly confers upon every defendant in a criminal trial the right "to be confronted with the witnesses against him" and "to have compulsory process for obtaining witnesses in his favor." Moreover, the Fifth Amendment also guarantees that no person shall be deprived of liberty without due process of law. It is the manifest duty of the courts to vindicate those guarantees, and to accomplish that it is essential that all relevant and admissible evidence be produced.

In this case we must weigh the importance of the general privilege of confidentiality of Presidential communications in performance of the President's responsibilities against the inroads of such a privilege on the fair administration of criminal justice. The interest in preserving confidentiality is weighty indeed and entitled to great respect. However, we cannot conclude that advisers will be moved to temper the candor of their remarks by the infrequent occasions of disclosure because of the possibility that such conversations will be called for in the context of a criminal prosecution.

On the other hand, the allowance of the privilege to withhold evidence that is demonstrably relevant in a criminal trial would cut deeply into the guarantee of due process of law and gravely impair the basic function of the courts. A President's acknowledged need for confidentiality in the communications of his office is general in nature, whereas the constitutional need for production of relevant evidence in a criminal proceeding is specific and central to the fair adjudication of a particular criminal case in the administration of justice. Without access to specific facts a criminal prosecution may be totally frustrated. The President's broad interest in confidentiality of communications will not be [impaired] by disclosure of a limited number of conversations preliminarily shown to have some bearing on the pending criminal cases.

We conclude that when the ground for asserting privilege as to subpoenaed materials sought for use in a criminal trial is based only on the generalized interest in confidentiality, it cannot prevail over the fundamental demands of due process of law in the fair administration of criminal justice. The generalized assertion of privilege must yield to the demonstrated, specific need for evidence in a pending criminal trial.

We have earlier determined that the District Court did not err in authorizing the issuance of the subpoena. If a President concludes that compliance with a subpoena would be injurious to the public interest he may properly, as was done here, invoke a claim of privilege on the return of the subpoena. Upon receiving a claim of privilege from the Chief Executive, it became the further duty of the District Court to treat the subpoenaed material as presumptively privileged and to require the Special Prosecutor to demonstrate that the Presidential material was "essential to the justice of the [p]ending criminal] case."   Here the District Court treated the material as presumptively privileged, proceeded to find that the Special Prosecutor had made a sufficient showing . . . and ordered [a private] examination of the subpoenaed material. On the basis of our examination of the record we are unable to conclude that the District Court erred in ordering the inspection. Accordingly we affirm [uphold] the order of the District Court that subpoenaed materials be transmitted to that court.   We now turn to the important question of the District Court's responsibilities in conducting the . . . examination of Presidential materials or communications delivered under the compulsion of the subpoena. . . .

[T]he matter of implementation [will] rest with the District Court. . . . Statements that meet the test of admissibility and relevance must be isolated; all other material must be excised. At this stage the District Court is not limited to representations of the Special Prosecutor as to the evidence sought by the subpoena; the material will be available to the District Court. It is elementary that [private] inspection of evidence is always a procedure calling for scrupulous protection against any release or publication of material not found by the court, at that stage, probably admissible in evidence and relevant to the issues of the trial for which it is sought. That being true of an ordinary situation, it is obvious that the District Court has a very heavy responsibility to see to it that Presidential conversations, which are either not relevant or not admissible, are accorded that high degree of respect due the President of the United States. Chief Justice Marshall, sitting as a trial judge in the *Burr* case, was extraordinarily careful to point out that

> "[i]n no case of this kind would a court be required to proceed against the president as against an ordinary individual."

Marshall's statement cannot be read to mean in any sense that a President is above the law, but relates to the singularly unique role under Art. II of a President's communications and activities, related to the performance of duties under that Article. Moreover, a President's communications and activities encompass a vastly wider range of sensitive material than would be true of any "ordinary individual." It is therefore necessary in the public interest to afford Presidential confidentiality the greatest protection consistent with the fair administration of justice. The need for confidentiality even as to idle conversations with associates in which casual reference might be made concerning political leaders within the country or foreign statesmen is too obvious to call for further treatment. We have no doubt that the District Judge will at all times accord to Presidential records that high degree of deference suggested in *United States v. Burr*, and will discharge his responsibility to see to it that until released to the Special Prosecutor no [privately examined] material is revealed to anyone. This burden applies with even greater force to excised material; once the decision is made to excise, the material is restored to its privileged status and should be returned under seal of its lawful custodian. . . .

Affirmed.

CLEAR AND PRESENT DANGER

SCHENCK v. UNITED STATES

The United States entered World War One - the War To End All Wars - on April 6, 1917. Congress, shortly after declaring war, passed, on May 18, 1917, the Military Conscription Act, to draft men for the American Expeditionary Force preparing to fight in Europe.

On June 15, 1917 the Congress acted to prevent interference with the draft by passing the Espionage Act, which read in part: "[Whoever, when the United States is at war], shall willfully obstruct the recruiting or enlistment service of the United States . . . shall be punished by a fine of not more than $10,000 or imprisonment for not more than twenty years, or both."

Charles T. Schenck was the General Secretary of the Socialist Party headquartered in Philadelphia. The Socialist Party was opposed to America's entry into the war and to conscription. On August 20, 1917 Schenck and his "comrades" prepared to mail an anti-draft leaflet to men which read in part: "Assert Your Rights . . . . Do not submit to intimidation." The Socialist Party went on to call conscription an "infamous conspiracy" and a "monstrous wrong against humanity."

The police raided the Socialist Party Headquarters and arrested Schenck. He was indicted, tried, and convicted on three charges relating to the Espionage Act. The First Amendment, Schenck argued, granted him "total immunity" - an absolute guarantee of free speech - making the Espionage Act's restrictions unconstitutional. Schenck appealed his conviction to the United States Supreme Court. Oral arguments were heard by the Court January 9 and 10 and a decision was announced March 3, 1919 by Associate Justice Oliver Wendell Holmes.

The complete text of *Schenck v. United States* can be found in volume 249 of *United States Reports.*

SCHENCK v. UNITED STATES

MARCH 3, 1919

JUSTICE OLIVER WENDELL HOLMES delivered the opinion of the Court: This is an indictment in three counts [three-part charge]. The first charges a conspiracy to violate the Espionage Act of June 15, 1917 . . . by causing and attempting to cause insubordination, etc., in the military and naval forces of the United States, and to obstruct the recruiting and enlistment service of the United States, when the United States was at war with the German Empire; to wit, that the defendant [Charles T. Schenck] wilfully conspired to have printed and circulated to men who had been called and accepted for military service under the Act of May 18, 1917, a document set forth and alleged to be calculated to cause such insubordination and obstruction. The count alleges overt acts in pursuance of the conspiracy, ending in the distribution of the document set forth. The second count alleges a conspiracy to commit an offense against the United States; to wit, to use the mails for the transmission of matter declared to be non-mailable by . . . the Act of June 15, 1917, to wit, the above-mentioned document. . . . The third count charges an unlawful use of the mails for the transmission of the same matter and otherwise as above. The [defendant was] found guilty on all the counts. [He] set up the First Amendment to the Constitution, forbidding Congress to make any law abridging the freedom of speech or of the press, and, bringing the case here on that ground, [has] argued some other points also of which we must dispose.

It is argued that the evidence, if admissible, was not sufficient to prove that the defendant Schenck was concerned in sending the documents. According to the testimony Schenck said he was general secretary of the Socialist party and had charge of the Socialist headquarters from which the documents were sent. He identified a book found there as the minutes of the executive committee of the party. The book showed a resolution of August 13, 1917, that 15,000 leaflets should be printed on the other side of one of them in use, to be mailed to men who had passed exemption boards, and for distribution. Schenck personally attended to the printing. On August 20 the general secretary's report said, "Obtained new leaflets from the printer and started work addressing envelopes," etc.; and there was a resolve that Comrade Schenck be allowed $125 for sending leaflets through the mail. He said that he had about fifteen or sixteen thousand printed. There were files of the circular in question in the inner office which he said were printed on the other side of the one-sided circular and were there for distribution. Other copies were proved to have been sent through the mails to drafted men. . . . [N]o reasonable man could doubt that the defendant Schenck was largely instrumental in sending the circulars about. . . .

It is objected that the documentary evidence was not admissible, because obtained upon a search warrant, valid, so far as appears. The contrary is established. The search warrant did not issue against the defendant, but against the Socialist headquarters at 1326 Arch street, and it would seem that the documents technically were not even in the defendant's possession. . . . [T]he notion that evidence even directly proceeding from the defendant in a criminal proceeding is excluded in all cases by the Fifth Amendment is plainly unsound.

The document in question, upon its first printed side, recited the first section of the Thirteenth Amendment, said that the idea embodied in it was violated by the Conscription Act, and that a conscript is little better than a convict. In impassioned language it intimated that conscription was despotism in its worst form and a monstrous wrong against humanity, in the interest of Wall street's chosen few. It said: "Do not submit to intimidation;" but in form at least confined itself to peaceful measures, such as a petition for the repeal of the act. The other and later printed side of the sheet was headed, "Assert Your Rights." It stated reasons for alleging that anyone violated the Constitution when he refused to recognize "your right to assert your opposition to the draft," and went on: "If you do not assert and support your rights, you are helping to deny or disparage rights which it is the solemn duty of all citizens and residents of the United States to retain." It described the arguments on the other side as coming from cunning politicians and a mercenary capitalist press, and even silent consent to the Conscription Law as helping to support an infamous conspiracy. It denied the power to send our citizens away to foreign shores to shoot up the people of other lands, and added that words could not express the condemnation such cold-blooded ruthlessness deserves, etc., etc., winding up, "You must do your share to maintain, support, and uphold the rights of the people of this country." Of course the document would not have been sent unless it had been intended to have some effect, and we do not see what effect it could be expected to have upon persons subject to the draft except to influence them to obstruct the carrying of it out. The defendants do not deny that the jury might find against them on this point.

But it is said, suppose that that was the tendency of this circular, it is protected by the First Amendment to the Constitution. . . . We admit that in many places and in ordinary times the [defendant], in saying all that was said in the circular, would have been within [his] constitutional rights. But the character of every act depends upon the circumstances in which it is done. The most stringent protection of free speech would not protect a man in falsely shouting fire in a theater, and causing a panic. It does not even protect a man from an injunction [order to stop] against uttering words that may have all the effect of force. The question in every case is whether the words used are used in such circumstances and are of such a nature as to create a clear and present danger that they will bring about the substantive evils that Congress has a right to prevent. It is a question of proximity and degree. When a nation is at war many things that might be said in time of peace are such a hindrance to its effort that their utterance will not be endured so long as men fight, and that no court could regard them as protected by any constitutional right. It seems to be admitted that if an actual obstruction of the recruiting service were proved, liability for words that produced that effect might be enforced. The Statute of 1917 . . . punishes conspiracies to obstruct as well as actual obstruction. If the act (speaking, or circulating a paper), its tendency and the intent with which it is done, are the same, we perceive no ground for saying that success alone warrants making the act a crime. . . . But as the right to free speech was not referred to specially, we have thought fit to add a few words.

It is not argued that a conspiracy to obstruct the draft was not within the words of the Act of 1917. The words are, 'obstruct the recruiting or enlistment service;' and it might be suggested that they refer only to making it hard to get volunteers. Recruiting heretofore usually having been accomplished by getting volunteers, the word is apt to call up that method only in our minds. But recruiting is gaining fresh supplies for the forces, as well by draft as otherwise. It is put as an alternative to enlistment or voluntary enrolment in this act. The fact that the Act of 1917 was enlarged by the amending Act of May 16, 1918, . . . of course, does not affect the present indictment, and would not, even if the former act had been repealed.

Judgments affirmed.

FORCED STERILIZATION

BUCK v. BELL

An Act of the Commonwealth of Virginia dated March 24, 1924 allowed the superintendents of certain state mental institutions, for the welfare of society and the health of the patient, to order the sterilization of male and female "mental defectives" with hereditary forms of insanity or imbecility.

In 1924, pursuant to the Virginia Sterilization Act, Carrie Buck, an eighteen-year-old "feeble-minded white woman," daughter of a feeble-minded mother and mother of an illegitimate, feeble-minded child, an inmate of the Virginia Colony for Epileptics and Feeble Minded, was ordered by the superintendent of that institution, J.H. Bell, to undergo sterilization surgery.

Attempting to prevent abuse of the sterilization statute, the law provided for administrative hearings within the State Colony to be attended by the inmate and his or her court-appointed guardian. The law also allowed appeal of the decision to the courts of Virginia.

Carrie Buck, ordered to undergo sterilization surgery by the Supervisor of the State Colony in 1924, fought the decision in an administrative hearing before the Directors of the State Colony and, when unsuccessful, appealed the decision to the Virginia Circuit Court, the Virginia Supreme Court of Appeals, and, finally, in 1927 to the United States Supreme Court.

Oral arguments where heard before the Court on April 27, 1927 and a decision was announced on May 2, 1927 by Associate Justice Oliver Wendell Holmes.

The complete text of *Buck v. Bell* can be found in volume 274 of *United States Reports.*

BUCK v. BELL

MAY 2, 1927

JUSTICE OLIVER WENDELL HOLMES delivered the opinion of the Court: This [case deals with] the superintendent of the State Colony for Epileptics and Feeble Minded, [J.H. Bell, who] was ordered to perform the operation of salpingectomy upon Carrie Buck . . . for the purpose of making her sterile. The case comes here upon the contention that the statute authorizing the judgment is void under the Fourteenth Amendment as denying to [Buck] due process of law and the equal protection of the laws.

Carrie Buck is a feeble minded white woman who was committed to the State Colony above mentioned. . . . She is the daughter of a feeble minded mother in the same institution, and the mother of an illegitimate feeble minded child. She was eighteen years old at the time of the trial of her case in the circuit court, in the latter part of 1924. An Act of Virginia approved March 20, 1924, recites that the health of the patient and the welfare of society may be promoted in certain cases by the sterilization of mental defectives, under careful safeguard, etc.; that the sterilization may be effected in males by vasectomy and in females by salpingectomy, without serious pain or substantial danger to life; that the Commonwealth is supporting in various institutions many defective persons who if now discharged would become a menace but if incapable of procreating might be discharged with safety and become self-supporting with benefit to themselves and to society; and that experience has shown that heredity plays an important part in the

transmission of insanity, imbecility, etc. The statute then
enacts that whenever the superintendent of certain
institutions including the above named State Colony shall
be of opinion that it is for the best interests of the
patients and of society that an inmate under his care
should be sexually sterilized, he may have the operation
performed upon any patient afflicted with hereditary
forms of insanity, imbecility, etc., on complying with the
very careful provisions by which the act protects the
patients from possible abuse.

The superintendent first presents a petition to the special
board of directors of his hospital or colony, stating the
facts and the grounds for his opinion, verified by
affidavit. Notice of the petition and of the time and place
of the hearing in the institution is to be served upon the
inmate, and also upon his guardian, and if there is no
guardian the superintendent is to apply to the circuit
court of the county to appoint one. If the inmate is a
minor notice also is to be given to his parents if any with
a copy of the petition. The board is to see to it that the
inmate may attend the hearings if desired by him or his
guardian. The evidence is all to be reduced to writing,
and after the board has made its order for or against the
operation, the superintendent, or the inmate, or his
guardian, may appeal to the circuit court of the county.
The circuit court may consider the record of the board
and the evidence before it and such other admissible
evidence as may be offered, and may affirm [uphold],
revise, or reverse the order of the board and enter such
order as it deems just. Finally any party may apply to the
supreme court of appeals. . . . There can be no doubt that
so far as procedure is concerned the rights of the patient
are most carefully considered, and as every step in this
case was taken in scrupulous compliance with the statute

and after months of observation, there is no doubt that in that respect [Buck] has had due process of law.

The attack is not upon the procedure but upon the substantive [essential] law. It seems to be contended that in no circumstances could such an order be justified. It certainly is contended that the order cannot be justified upon the existing grounds. . . . The judgment finds . . . that Carrie Buck "is the probable potential parent of socially inadequate offspring, likewise afflicted, that she may be sexually sterilized without detriment to her general health and that her welfare and that of society will be promoted by her sterilization." . . . We have seen more than once that the public welfare may call upon the best citizens for their lives. It would be strange if it could not call upon those who already sap the strength of the state for these lesser sacrifices, often not felt to be such by those concerned, in order to prevent our being swamped with incompetence. It is better for all the world, if instead of waiting to execute degenerate offspring for crime, or to let them starve for their imbecility, society can prevent those who are manifestly unfit from continuing their kind. The principle that sustains [upholds] compulsory vaccination is broad enough to cover cutting the Fallopian tubes. Three generations of imbeciles are enough.

But, it is said, however it might be if this reasoning were applied generally, it fails when it is confined to the small number who are in the institutions named and is not applied to the multitudes outside. It is the usual last resort of constitutional arguments to point out shortcomings of this sort. But the answer is that the law does all that is needed when it does all that it can, indicates a policy, applies it to all within the lines, and seeks to bring within the lines all similarly situated so far and so fast as its means allow. Of course so far as the operations enable those who otherwise must be kept confined to be returned to the world, and thus open the asylum to others, the equality aimed at will be more nearly reached.

Judgment affirmed [upheld].

MOB JUSTICE

SCOTTSBORO BOYS v. ALABAMA

On March 25, 1931 nine "Negro boys" - Clarence Norris, Olen Montgomery, Ozie Powell, Haywood Patterson, Willie Roberson, Charlie Weems, Eugene Williams, and Roy and Andy Wright - all nineteen years of age and under - were taken off a train in Northern Alabama by a sheriff's posse and brought to Scottsboro, Alabama, where they were charged with the rape of two white women.

The "Scottsboro Boys" were never asked whether they had or were able to employ legal counsel, or wished to have legal counsel appointed, or whether they had friends or family who might assist in obtaining legal counsel for them. Most were under-age, all were poor, illiterate, and from out of state. Until the very morning of their trials, no legal counsel had even been named to defend them.

In a hostile "mob justice" atmosphere in which the State Militia had to be called out to protect them from a lynch mob, the Scottsboro Boys were tried before Jackson County Circuit Court Judge Alfred E. Hawkins and an all-white jury. On April 9, 1931, at the end of a one-day trial, all but one of the Scottsboro Boys were sentenced to die on July 10, 1931 in Alabama's electric chair.

Their convictions and death sentences were appealed to the Alabama Supreme Court. Writing for the majority, Chief Justice Anderson of the Alabama Supreme Court reversed the conviction of one and affirmed the convictions and death sentences of seven others. A review based on the rights of those accused of crimes to legal counsel was granted by the U.S. Supreme Court. Oral arguments were heard before the Court on October 10, 1932 and a decision was announced November 7, 1932 by Associate Justice George Sutherland.

The complete text of *Scottsboro Boys v. Alabama* can be found in volume 287 of *United States Reports*.

SCOTTSBORO BOYS v. ALABAMA

NOVEMBER 7, 1932

JUSTICE GEORGE SUTHERLAND delivered the opinion of the Court: .... The petitioners [Ozie Powell, Willie Roberson, Andy Wright, Olen Montgomery, Haywood Patterson, Charley Weems, and Clarence Norris], hereinafter referred to as defendants, are negroes charged with the crime of rape, committed upon the persons of two white girls. The crime is said to have been committed on March 25, 1931. The indictment [charge] was returned in a state court . . . on March 31, and the record recites that on the same day the defendants were arraigned [brought before the court] and entered pleas of not guilty. There is a further recital to the effect that upon the arraignment they were represented by counsel. But no counsel had been employed, and aside from a statement made by the trial judge several days later during a [discussion] immediately preceding the trial, the record does not disclose when, or under what circumstances, an appointment of counsel was made, or who was appointed. . . . [T]he trial judge, in response to a question, said that he had appointed all the members of the bar for the purpose of arraigning the defendants and then of course anticipated that the members of the bar would continue to help the defendants if no counsel appeared. Upon the argument here both sides accepted that as a correct statement of the facts concerning the matter.

. . . . [T]he defendants were tried in three [separate] groups. . . . As each of the three cases was called for trial, each defendant was arraigned, and, having the indictment read to him, entered a plea of not guilty. Whether the original arraignment and pleas were regarded as ineffective is not shown. Each of the three trials was completed within a single day. Under the Alabama statute the punishment for rape is to be fixed by the jury, and in its discretion may be from ten years' imprisonment to death. The juries found defendants guilty and imposed the death penalty upon all. The trial court overruled motions for new trials and sentenced the defendants in accordance with the verdicts. The judgments were affirmed [upheld] by the state supreme court. Chief Justice Anderson thought the defendants had not been accorded a fair trial and strongly dissented.

In this court the judgments are assailed upon the grounds that the defendants . . . were denied due process of law and the equal protection of the laws, in [violation] of the Fourteenth Amendment, specifically as follows: (1) they were not given a fair, impartial and deliberate trial; (2) they were denied the right of counsel, with the accustomed incidents of consultation and opportunity of preparation for trial; and (3) they were tried before juries from which qualified members of their own race were systematically excluded. . . .

The only one of the assignments which we shall consider is the second, in respect of the denial of counsel. . . .

The record shows that on the day when the offense is said to have been committed, these defendants, together with a number of other negroes, were upon a freight train on its way through Alabama. On the same train were seven white boys and the two white girls. A fight took place between the negroes and the white boys, in the course of which the white boys, with the exception of one named Gilley, were thrown off the train. A message was sent ahead, reporting the fight and asking that every negro be gotten off the train. The participants in the fight, and the two girls, were in an open gondola car. The two girls testified that each of them was assaulted by six different negroes in turn, and they identified the seven defendants as having been among the number. None of the white boys was called to testify, with the exception of Gilley, who was called in rebuttal [an attempt to produce evidence to the contrary].

Before the train reached Scottsboro, Alabama, a sheriff's posse seized the defendants and two other negroes. Both girls and the negroes then were taken to Scottsboro, the county seat. Word of their coming and of the alleged assault had preceded them, and they were met at Scottsboro by a large crowd. It does not sufficiently appear that the defendants were seriously threatened with, or that they were actually in danger of, mob violence; but it does appear that the attitude of the community was one of great hostility. The sheriff thought it necessary to call for the militia to assist in safeguarding the prisoners. Chief Justice Anderson pointed out in his opinion that every step taken from the arrest and arraignment to the sentence was accompanied by the military. Soldiers took the defendants to Gadsden for safekeeping, brought them back to Scottsboro for arraignment, returned them to Gadsden for safekeeping while awaiting trial, escorted them to Scottsboro for trial a few days later, and guarded the court house and grounds at every stage of the proceedings. It is perfectly apparent that the proceedings, from beginning to end, took place in an atmosphere of tense, hostile and excited public sentiment. During the entire time, the defendants were closely confined or were under military guard. The record does not disclose their ages, except that one of them was nineteen; but the record

clearly indicates that most, if not all, of them were
youthful, and they are constantly referred to as "the
boys." They were ignorant and illiterate. All of them
were residents of other states, where alone members of
their families or friends resided.

However guilty [the] defendants, upon due inquiry might
prove to have been, they were, until convicted, presumed
to be innocent. It was the duty of the court having their
cases in charge to see that they were denied no necessary
incident of a fair trial. . . . The sole inquiry which we are
permitted to make is whether the federal Constitution was
[violated]; and as to that, we confine ourselves, as already
suggested to the inquiry whether the defendants were in
substance denied the right of counsel, and if so, whether
such denial infringes the due process clause of the
Fourteenth Amendment.

First. The record shows that immediately upon the return
of the indictment defendants were arraigned and pleaded
not guilty. Apparently they were not asked whether they
had, or were able to employ, counsel, or wished to have
counsel appointed; or whether they had friends or
relatives who might assist in that regard if communicated
with. That it would not have been an idle ceremony to
have given the defendants reasonable opportunity to
communicate with their families and endeavor to obtain
counsel is demonstrated by the fact that very soon after
conviction able counsel appeared in their behalf. This was
pointed out by Chief Justice Anderson in the course of his
dissenting opinion. "They were nonresidents," he said,
"and had little time or opportunity to get in touch with
their families and friends who were scattered throughout
two other states, and time has demonstrated that they
could or would have been represented by able counsel had

a better opportunity been given by a reasonable delay in the trial of the cases judging from the number and activity of counsel that appeared immediately or shortly after their conviction."

It is hardly necessary to say that the right to counsel being conceded, a defendant should be afforded a fair opportunity to secure counsel of his own choice. Not only was that not done here, but such designation of counsel as was attempted was either so indefinite or so close upon the trial as to amount to a denial of effective and substantial aid in that regard. This will be amply demonstrated by a brief review of the record.

April 6, six days after indictment, the trials began. When the first case was called, the court inquired whether the parties were ready for trial. The state's attorney replied that he was ready to proceed. No one answered for the defendants or appeared to represent or defend them. Mr. Roddy, a Tennessee lawyer not a member of the local bar, addressed the court, saying that he had not been employed, but that people who were interested had spoken to him about the case. He was asked by the court whether he intended to appear for the defendants, and answered that he would like to appear along with counsel that the court might appoint.

. . . . [I]n this casual fashion the matter of counsel in a capital case [one in which the death penalty may be imposed] was disposed of.

It thus will be seen that until the very morning of the trial no lawyer had been named or definitely designated to represent the defendants. Prior to that time, the trial judge had "appointed all the members of the bar" for the

limited "purpose of arraigning the defendants." Whether
they would represent the defendants thereafter if no
counsel appeared in their behalf, was a matter of
speculation only, or, as the judge indicated, of mere
anticipation on the part of the court. Such a designation,
even if made for all purposes, would, in our opinion, have
fallen far short of meeting, in any proper sense, a
requirement for the appointment of counsel. How many
lawyers were members of the bar does not appear; but, in
the very nature of things, whether many or few, they
would not, thus collectively named, have been given that
clear appreciation of responsibility or impressed with that
individual sense of duty which should and naturally
would accompany the appointment of a selected member
of the bar, specifically named and assigned.

That this action of the trial judge in respect of
appointment of counsel was little more than an expansive
gesture, imposing no substantial or definite obligation
upon any one, is borne out by the fact that prior to the
calling of the case for trial on April 6, a leading member
of the local bar accepted employment on the side of the
prosecution and actively participated in the trial. It is
true that he said that before doing so he had understood
Mr. Roddy would be employed as counsel for the
defendants. This the lawyer in question, of his own
accord, frankly stated to the court; and no doubt he acted
with the utmost good faith. Probably other members of
the bar had a like understanding. In any event, the
circumstance lends emphasis to the conclusion that during
perhaps the most critical period of the proceedings against
these defendants, that is to say, from the time of their
arraignment until the beginning of their trial, when
consultation, thorough-going investigation and preparation
were vitally important, the defendants did not have the

aid of counsel in any real sense, although they were as much entitled to such aid during that period as at the trial itself.

Nor do we think the situation was helped by what occurred on the morning of the trial. At that time ... Mr. Roddy stated to the court that he did not appear as counsel, but that he would like to appear along with counsel that the court might appoint; that he had not been given an opportunity to prepare the case; that he was not familiar with the procedure in Alabama, but merely came down as a friend of the people who were interested; that he thought the boys would be better off if he should step entirely out of the case. Mr. Moody, a member of the local bar, expressed a willingness to help Mr. Roddy in anything he could do under the circumstances. To this the court responded, "All right, all the lawyers that will; of course I would not require a lawyer to appear if - ." And Mr. Moody continued, "I am willing to do that for him as a member of the bar; I will go ahead and help do anything I can do." With this dubious understanding, the trials immediately proceeded. The defendants, young, ignorant, illiterate, surrounded by hostile sentiment, haled back and forth under guard of soldiers, charged with an atrocious crime regarded with especial horror in the community where they were to be tried, were thus put in peril of their lives within a few moments after counsel for the first time charged with any degree of responsibility began to represent them.

It is not enough to assume that counsel thus precipitated into the case thought there was no defense, and exercised their best judgment in proceeding to trial without preparation. Neither they nor the court could say what a prompt and thorough-going investigation might disclose as to the facts. No attempt was made to investigate. No opportunity to do so was given. Defendants were immediately hurried to trial. Chief Justice Anderson, after disclaiming any intention to criticize harshly counsel who attempted to represent defendants at the trials, said: "The record indicates that the appearance was rather pro forma [routine] than zealous and active." Under the circumstances disclosed, we hold that defendants were not accorded the right of counsel in any substantial sense. To decide otherwise, would simply be to ignore actualities. . . .

It is true that great and inexcusable delay in the enforcement of our criminal law is one of the grave evils of our time. Continuances [postponements] are frequently granted for unnecessarily long periods of time, and delays [for] . . . motions [requests] for new trial and hearings upon appeal have come in many cases to be a distinct reproach to the administration of justice. The prompt disposition of criminal cases is to be commended and encouraged. But in reaching that result a defendant, charged with a serious crime, must not be stripped of his right to have sufficient time to advise with counsel and prepare his defense. To do that is not to proceed promptly in the calm spirit of regulated justice but to go forward with the haste of the mob.

As the court said in *Com. v. O'Keefe*,

> "It is vain to give the accused a day in court, with no opportunity to prepare for it, or to guarantee him counsel without giving the latter any opportunity to acquaint himself with the facts or law of the case."

[And in *Reliford v. State*]

> "A prompt and vigorous administration of the
> criminal law is commendable and we have no
> desire to clog the wheels of justice. What we
> here decide is that to force a defendant, charged
> with a serious misdemeanor, to trial within five
> hours of his arrest, is not due process of law,
> regardless of the merits of the case."

Second. The Constitution of Alabama provides that in all
criminal prosecutions the accused shall enjoy the right to
have the assistance of counsel; and a state statute requires
the court in a capital case, where the defendant is unable
to employ counsel, to appoint counsel for him. The state
supreme court held that these provisions had not been
infringed, and with that holding we are powerless to
interfere. The question, however, which it is our duty,
and within our power, to decide, is whether the denial of
the assistance of counsel [violates] the due process clause
of the Fourteenth Amendment to the federal Constitution.

. . . . [H]ow can a judge, whose functions are purely
judicial, effectively discharge the obligations of counsel
for the accused? He can and should see to it that in the
proceedings before the court the accused shall be dealt
with justly and fairly. He cannot investigate the facts,
advise and direct the defense, or participate in those
necessary conferences between counsel and accused which
sometimes partake of the inviolable character of the
confessional.

. . . . It . . . appears that in at least twelve of the thirteen
colonies . . . the right to counsel [was] fully recognized in
all criminal prosecutions, save that in one or two instances

the right was limited to capital offenses or to the more
serious crimes. . . .

The Sixth Amendment . . . provides that in all criminal
prosecutions the accused shall enjoy the right "to have the
assistance of counsel for his defense."

. . . . [T]his court has considered that freedom of speech
and of the press are rights protected by the due process
clause of the Fourteenth Amendment, although in the
First Amendment, Congress is prohibited in specific terms
from abridging the right.

. . . . The rule is an aid to construction, and in some
instances may be conclusive; but it must yield to more
compelling considerations whenever such considerations
exist.   The fact that the right involved is of such a
character that it cannot be denied without violating those
"fundamental principles of liberty and justice which lie at
the base of all our civil and political institutions" is
obviously one of those compelling considerations which
must prevail in determining whether it is embraced within
the due process clause of the Fourteenth Amendment,
although it be specifically dealt with in another part of
the federal Constitution. . . . [I]n *Twining v. New Jersey*,
Justice Moody, speaking for the court, said that " . . . it is
possible that some of the personal rights safeguarded by
the first eight Amendments against national action may
also be safeguarded against state action, because a denial
of them would be a denial of due process of law. If this is
so, it is not because those rights are enumerated in the
first eight Amendments, but because they are of such a
nature that they are included in the conception of due
process of law."   While the question has never been
categorically determined by this court, a consideration of

the nature of the right and a review of the expressions of
this and other courts, make it clear that the right to the
aid of counsel is of this fundamental character.

It never has been doubted by this court, or any other so
far as we know, that notice and hearing are preliminary
steps essential to the passing of an enforceable judgment,
and that they, together with a legally competent tribunal
having jurisdiction of the case, constitute basic elements
of the constitutional requirement of due process of law.
The words of Webster, so often quoted, that by "the law
of the land" is intended "a law which hears before it
condemns," have been repeated in varying forms of
expression in a multitude of decisions. . . .

Justice Field, in . . . *Galpin v. Page,* said that the rule that
no one shall be personally bound until he has had his day
in court was as old as the law, and it meant that he must
be cited [summoned] to appear and afforded an
opportunity to be heard. . . .

What, then, does a hearing include? Historically and in
practice, in our own country at least, it has always
included the right to the aid of counsel when desired and
provided by the party asserting the right. The right to be
heard would be, in many cases, of little avail if it did not
comprehend the right to be heard by counsel. Even the
intelligent and educated layman has small and sometimes
no skill in the science of law. If charged with crime, he is
incapable, generally, of determining for himself whether
the indictment is good or bad. . . . Left without the aid of
counsel he may be put on trial without a proper charge,
and convicted upon incompetent evidence, or evidence
irrelevant to the issue or otherwise inadmissible. He lacks
both the skill and knowledge adequately to prepare his

defense, even though he have a perfect one. He requires the guiding hand of counsel at every step in the proceedings against him. Without it, though he be not guilty, he faces the danger of conviction because he does not know how to establish his innocence. If that be true of men of intelligence, how much more true is it of the ignorant and illiterate, or those of feeble intellect. If in any case, civil or criminal, a state or federal court were arbitrarily to refuse to hear a party by counsel, employed by and appearing for him, it reasonably may not be doubted that such a refusal would be a denial of a hearing, and, therefore, of due process in the constitutional sense.

. . . . In the light of the facts outlined in the forepart of this opinion - the ignorance and illiteracy of the defendants, their youth, the circumstances of public hostility, the imprisonment and the close surveillance of the defendants by the military forces, the fact that their friends and families were all in other states and communication with them necessarily difficult, and above all that they stood in deadly peril of their lives - we think the failure of the trial court to give them reasonable time and opportunity to secure counsel was a clear denial of due process.

But passing that, and assuming their inability, even if opportunity had been given, to employ counsel, as the trial court evidently did assume, we are of opinion that, under the circumstances just stated, the necessity of counsel was so vital and imperative that the failure of the trial court to make an effective appointment of counsel was likewise a denial of due process within the meaning of the Fourteenth Amendment. Whether this would be so in other criminal prosecutions, or under other circumstances, we need not determine. All that it is necessary now to decide, as we do decide, is that in a capital case, where the defendant is unable to employ counsel, and is incapable adequately of making his own defense because of ignorance, feeblemindedness, illiteracy, or the like, it is the duty of the court, whether requested or not, to assign counsel for him as a necessary requisite of due process of law; and that duty is not discharged by an assignment at such a time or under such circumstances as to preclude the giving of effective aid in the preparation and trial of the case. To hold otherwise would be to ignore the fundamental [proposition] "that there are certain immutable principles of justice which inhere in the very idea of free government which no member of the Union may disregard." In a case such as this, whatever may be the rule in other cases, the right to have counsel appointed, when necessary, [logically follows] from the constitutional right to be heard by counsel.

In *Hendryx v. State*, there was no statute authorizing the assignment of an attorney to defend an indigent person accused of crime, but the court held that such an assignment was necessary to accomplish the ends of public justice, and that the court possessed the inherent power to make it. "Where a prisoner," the court said, "without legal knowledge, is confined in jail, absent from his friends, without the aid of legal advice or the means of investigating the charge against him, it is impossible to conceive of a fair trial where he is compelled to conduct his cause in court, without the aid of counsel. . . .

Let us suppose the extreme case of a prisoner charged with a capital offense, who is deaf and dumb, illiterate and feeble-minded, unable to employ counsel, with the whole power of the state arrayed against him, prosecuted by counsel for the state without assignment of counsel for his defense, tried, convicted and sentenced to death. Such a result, which, if carried into execution, would be little short of judicial murder, it cannot be doubted would be a gross violation of the guaranty of due process of law; and we venture to think that no appellate court, state or federal, would hesitate so to decide. The duty of the trial court to appoint counsel under such circumstances is clear, as it is clear under circumstances such as are disclosed by the record here; and its power to do so, even in the absence of a statute, can not be questioned. Attorneys are officers of the court, and are bound to render service when required by such an appointment.

The United States by statute and every state in the Union by express provision of law, or by the determination of its courts, make it the duty of the trial judge, where the accused is unable to employ counsel, to appoint counsel for him. In most states the rule applies broadly to all criminal prosecutions, in others it is limited to the more serious crimes, and in a very limited number, to capital cases. A rule adopted with such unanimous accord reflects, if it does not establish the inherent right to have counsel appointed at least in cases like the present, and lends convincing support to the conclusion we have reached as to the fundamental nature of that right.

The judgments must be reversed and the causes remanded [returned to the lower court] for further proceedings not inconsistent with this opinion.

Judgments reversed.

PLEDGE OF ALLEGIANCE

MINERSVILLE SCHOOL DISTRICT v. GOBITIS

In 1935 twelve-year-old Lillian Gobitis and her ten-year-old brother, William, students in a Minersville, Pennsylvania public school, were expelled for insubordination for refusing to participate in the state-mandated daily pledge of allegiance to the flag.

Lillian and William, who stood in respectful silence while their classmates recited the pledge, were members of the Jehovah's Witnesses. They held the strong and sincere religious conviction, as expressed in 20 Exodus 3 through 5, that saluting the flag would force them to violate the law of God.

Pennsylvania made participation in the flag salute mandatory for all students and expelled all students who, like Lillian and William, would not comply. Walter Gobitis, on behalf of his children, challenged the Pennsylvania Pledge Law. Claiming an infringement of his children's constitutional right to the free exercise of their religion, the elder Gobitis, with the assistance of the ACLU, asked a U.S. District Court to stop the School Board from forcing his children to recite the pledge as a condition of their continued attendance in a public school.

On June 18, 1938 the U.S. District Court found in favor of the Gobitis children. The School Board appealed. On November 10, 1939 the U.S. Court of Appeals affirmed the lower court's decision. The School Board appealed again. On March 4, 1940 the United States Supreme Court agreed to a review.

Oral arguments were heard on April 25 and a decision was announced on June 3, 1940 by Associate Justice Felix Frankfurter.

The complete text of *Minersville School District v Gobitis* can be found in volume 310 of *United States Reports.*

MINERSVILLE SCHOOL DISTRICT v. GOBITIS

JUNE 3, 1940

JUSTICE FELIX FRANKFURTER delivered the opinion of the Court: A grave responsibility confronts this Court whenever in course of litigation it must reconcile the conflicting claims of liberty and authority. But when the liberty invoked is liberty of conscience, and the authority is authority to safeguard the nation's fellowship, judicial conscience is put to its severest test. Of such a nature is the present controversy.

Lillian Gobitis, aged twelve, and her brother, William, aged ten, were expelled from the public schools of Minersville, Pennsylvania, for refusing to salute the national flag as part of a daily school exercise. The local Board of Education required both teachers and pupils to participate in this ceremony. The ceremony is a familiar one. The right hand is placed on the breast and the following pledge recited in unison: "I pledge allegiance to my flag, and to the Republic for which it stands; one nation indivisible, with liberty and justice for all." While the words are spoken, teachers and pupils extend their right hands in salute to the flag. The Gobitis family are affiliated with "Jehovah's Witnesses," for whom the Bible as the Word of God is the supreme authority. The children had been brought up conscientiously to believe that such a gesture of respect for the flag was forbidden by command of scripture.

The Gobitis children were of an age for which Pennsylvania makes school attendance compulsory. Thus

they were denied a free education, and their parents had
to put them into private schools. To be relieved of the
financial burden thereby entailed, their father, on behalf
of the children and in his own behalf, brought this suit.
He sought to enjoin [stop] the authorities from continuing
to exact participation in the flag-salute ceremony as a
condition of his children's attendance at the Minersville
school. After trial of the issues, Judge Maris [issued the
injunction] in the District Court, on the basis of a
thoughtful opinion, at a preliminary stage of the
litigation; his decree was affirmed [upheld] by the Circuit
Court of Appeals. Since this decision ran counter to
several per curiam [by the whole court, without one
author] dispositions of this Court, we granted certiorari
[agreed to hear the case] to give the matter full
reconsideration. . . . [T]he Committee on the Bill of
Rights of the American Bar Association and the American
Civil Liberties Union, as friends of the Court, have helped
us to our conclusion.

We must decide whether the requirement of participation
in such a ceremony, exacted from a child who refuses
upon sincere religious grounds, infringes without due
process of law the liberty guaranteed by the Fourteenth
Amendment.

Centuries of strife over the erection of particular dogmas
as exclusive or all-comprehending faiths led to the
inclusion of a guarantee for religious freedom in the Bill
of Rights. The First Amendment, and the Fourteenth
through its absorption of the First, sought to guard against
repetition of those bitter religious struggles by
prohibiting the establishment of a state religion and by
securing to every sect the free exercise of its faith. So
pervasive is the acceptance of this precious right that its

scope is brought into question, as here, only when the conscience of individuals collides with the felt necessities of society.

Certainly the affirmative pursuit of one's convictions about the ultimate mystery of the universe and man's relation to it is placed beyond the reach of law. Government may not interfere with organized or individual expression of belief or disbelief. Propagation of belief - or even of disbelief in the supernatural - is protected, whether in church or chapel, mosque or synagogue, tabernacle or meeting-house. Likewise the Constitution assures generous immunity to the individual from imposition of penalties for offending, in the course of his own religious activities, the religious views of others, be they a minority or those who are dominant in government.

But the manifold character of man's relations may bring his conception of religious duty into conflict with the secular interests of his fellow-men. When does the constitutional guarantee compel exemption from doing what society thinks necessary for the promotion of some great common end, or from a penalty for conduct which appears dangerous to the general good? To state the problem is to recall the truth that no single principle can answer all of life's complexities. The right to freedom of religious belief, however dissident and however obnoxious to the cherished beliefs of others - even of a majority - is itself the denial of an absolute. But to affirm that the freedom to follow conscience has itself no limits in the life of a society would deny that very plurality of principles which, as a matter of history, underlies protection of religious toleration. Our present task then, as so often the case with courts, is to reconcile two rights in order to prevent either from destroying the other. But, because in safeguarding conscience we are dealing with interests so subtle and so dear, every possible leeway should be given to the claims of religious faith.

In the judicial enforcement of religious freedom we are concerned with a historic concept. The religious liberty which the Constitution protects has never excluded legislation of general scope not directed against doctrinal loyalties of particular sects. Judicial nullification of legislation cannot be justified by attributing to the framers of the Bill of Rights views for which there is no historic warrant. Conscientious scruples have not, in the course of the long struggle for religious toleration, relieved the individual from obedience to a general law not aimed at the promotion or restriction of religious beliefs. The mere possession of religious convictions which contradict the relevant concerns of a political society does not relieve the citizen from the discharge of political responsibilities. The necessity for this adjustment has again and again been recognized. In a number of situations the exertion of political authority has been sustained [upheld], while basic considerations of religious freedom have been left inviolate. In all these cases the general laws in question, upheld in their application to those who refused obedience from religious conviction, were manifestations of specific powers of government deemed by the legislature essential to secure and maintain that orderly, tranquil, and free society without which religious toleration itself is unattainable. Nor does the freedom of speech assured by Due Process move in a more absolute circle of immunity than that enjoyed by religious freedom. Even if it were assumed that freedom of speech goes beyond the historic concept of full opportunity to utter and to disseminate views, however heretical or offensive to dominant opinion, and includes freedom from conveying what may be deemed an implied but rejecting affirmation, the question remains whether school children, like the Gobitis children, must be excused from conduct required of all the other children in the promotion of national cohesion. We are dealing with an interest inferior to none in the hierarchy of legal values. National unity is the basis of national security. To deny the legislature the right to select appropriate means for its attainment presents a totally different order of problem from that of the propriety of subordinating the possible ugliness of littered streets to the free expression of opinion through distribution of handbills.

Situations like the present are phases of the profoundest problem confronting a democracy - the problem which Lincoln cast in memorable dilemma: "Must a government of necessity be too *strong* for the liberties of its people, or too *weak* to maintain its own existence?" No mere textual reading or logical talisman can solve the dilemma. And when the issue demands judicial determination, it is not the personal notion of judges of what wise adjustment requires which must prevail.

Unlike the instances we have cited, the case before us is not concerned with an exertion of legislative power for the promotion of some specific need or interest of secular society - the protection of the family, the promotion of health, the common defense, the raising of public revenues to defray the cost of government. But all these specific activities of government presuppose the existence of an organized political society. The ultimate foundation of a free society is the binding tie of cohesive sentiment. Such a sentiment is fostered by all those agencies of the mind and spirit which may serve to gather up the traditions of a people, transmit them from generation to generation, and thereby create that continuity of a treasured common life which constitutes a civilization. "We live by symbols." The flag is the symbol of our national unity, transcending all internal differences, however large, within the framework of the Constitution. This Court has had occasion to say that ". . . the flag is the symbol of the Nation's power, the emblem of freedom in its truest, best sense . . . it signifies government resting on the consent of the governed; liberty regulated by law; the protection of the weak against the strong; security against the exercise of arbitrary power; and absolute safety for free institutions against foreign aggression."

The case before us must be viewed as though the legislature of Pennsylvania had itself formally directed the flag-salute for the children of Minersville; had made no exemption for children whose parents were possessed of conscientious scruples like those of the Gobitis family; and had indicated its belief in the desirable ends to be secured by having its public school children share a common experience at those periods of development when their minds are supposedly receptive to its assimilation, by an exercise appropriate in time and place and setting, and one designed to evoke in them appreciation of the nation's hopes and dreams, its sufferings and sacrifices. The precise issue, then, for us to decide is whether the legislatures of the various states and the authorities in a thousand counties and school districts of this country are barred from determining the appropriateness of various means to evoke that unifying sentiment without which there can ultimately be no liberties, civil or religious. To stigmatize legislative judgment in providing for this universal gesture of respect for the symbol of our national life in the setting of the common school as a lawless inroad on that freedom of conscience which the Constitution protects, would amount to no less than the pronouncement of pedagogical and psychological dogma in a field where courts possess no marked and certainly no controlling competence. The influences which help toward a common feeling for the common country are manifold. Some may seem harsh and others no doubt are foolish. Surely, however, the end is legitimate. And the effective means for its attainment are still so uncertain and so unauthenticated by science as to preclude us from putting the widely prevalent belief in flag-saluting beyond the pale of legislative power. It mocks reason and denies our whole history to find in the allowance of a requirement to salute our flag on fitting occasions the seeds of sanction for obeisance to a leader.

The wisdom of training children in patriotic impulses by those compulsions which necessarily pervade so much of the educational process is not for our independent judgment. Even were we convinced of the folly of such a measure, such belief would be no proof of its unconstitutionality. For ourselves, we might be tempted to say that the deepest patriotism is best engendered by giving unfettered scope to the most crochety beliefs. Perhaps it is best, even from the standpoint of those interests which ordinances like the one under review seek to promote, to give to the least popular sect leave from conformities like those here in issue. But the courtroom is not the arena for debating issues of educational policy. It is not our province to choose among competing considerations in the subtle process of securing effective loyalty to the traditional ideals of democracy, while respecting at the same time individual idiosyncracies among a people so diversified in racial origins and religious allegiances. So to hold would in effect make us the school board for the country. That authority has not been given to this Court, nor should we assume it.

We are dealing here with the formative period in the development of citizenship. Great diversity of psychological and ethical opinion exists among us concerning the best way to train children for their place in society. Because of these differences and because of reluctance to permit a single, iron-cast system of education to be imposed upon a nation compounded of so many strains, we have held that, even though public education is one of our most cherished democratic institutions, the Bill of Rights bars a state from compelling all children to attend the public schools. But it is a very different thing for this Court to exercise censorship over the conviction of legislatures that a particular program or exercise will best promote in the minds of children who attend the common schools an attachment to the institutions of their country.

What the school authorities are really asserting is the right to awaken in the child's mind considerations as to the significance of the flag contrary to those implanted by the parent. In such an attempt the state is normally at a disadvantage in competing with the parent's authority, so long - and this is the vital aspect of religious toleration - as parents are unmolested in their right to counteract by their own persuasiveness the wisdom and rightness of those loyalties which the state's educational system is seeking to promote. Except where the transgression of constitutional liberty is too plain for argument, personal freedom is best maintained - so long as the remedial channels of the democratic process remain open and unobstructed - when it is ingrained in a people's habits and not enforced against popular policy by the coercion of adjudicated law. That the flag-salute is an allowable portion of a school program for those who do not invoke conscientious scruples is surely not debatable. But for us to insist that, though the ceremony may be required, exceptional immunity must be given to dissidents, is to maintain that there is no basis for a legislative judgment that such an exemption might introduce elements of difficulty into the school discipline, might cast doubts in the minds of the other children which would themselves weaken the effect of the exercise.

The preciousness of the family relation, the authority and independence which give dignity to parenthood, indeed the enjoyment of all freedom, presuppose the kind of ordered society which is summarized by our flag. A society which is dedicated to the preservation of these ultimate values of civilization may in self-protection utilize the educational process for inculcating those almost unconscious feelings which bind men together in a comprehending loyalty, whatever may be their lesser differences and difficulties. That is to say, the process may be utilized so long as men's right to believe as they please, to win others to their way of belief, and their right to assemble in their chosen places of worship for the devotional ceremonies of their faith, are all fully respected.

Judicial review, itself a limitation on popular government, is a fundamental part of our constitutional scheme. But to the legislature no less than to courts is committed the guardianship of deeply-cherished liberties. Where all the effective means of inducing political changes are left free from interference, education in the abandonment of foolish legislation is itself a training in liberty. To fight out the wise use of legislative authority in the forum of public opinion and before legislative assemblies rather than to transfer such a contest to the judicial arena, serves to vindicate the self-confidence of a free people.

Reversed.

PLEDGE OF ALLEGIANCE

BOARD OF EDUCATION v. BARNETTE

In January 1942 the West Virginia Board of Education, in compliance with the State Legislature, required classroom instruction in "Americanism" including, in all public, private, and parochial schools, a daily pledge of allegiance.

Failure of a student to recite the pledge was insubordination and resulted in expulsion. Expelled students were considered delinquent. Parents of delinquent students were liable for prosecution. Readmission could not be obtained without reciting the required pledge.

Walter Barnette, a West Virginia parent and a Jehovah's Witness, along with other adult Witnesses with school-age children, objected to the pledge requirement. The objections of the Witnesses, a religious group believing that the obligations imposed by the laws of God are superior to those imposed by the laws of men, were based on Exodus, Chapter 20, verses 4 and 5, which said: "Thou shalt not make unto thee any graven image, or any likeness of anything that is in heaven above or that is in earth beneath, or that is in water under the earth; thou shall not bow down thyself to them, nor serve them."

Barnette asked a Federal District Court to stop the Board of Education from punishing his children for their non-participation in the pledge of allegiance. The District Court refused and Barnette appealed to the U.S. Supreme Court to overrule their 1940 Jehovah's Witnesses v. Pledge of Allegiance decision in the *Gobitis* case.

Oral arguments were heard before the Court on March 11, 1943 and a decision was announced June 14, 1943 (Flag Day) by Associate Justice Robert Jackson.

The complete text of *Board of Education v Barnette* can be found in volume 310 of *United States Reports.*

BOARD OF EDUCATION v. BARNETTE

JUNE 14, 1943

JUSTICE ROBERT JACKSON delivered the opinion of the Court: Following the decision by this Court on June 3, 1940, in *Minersville School District v. Gobitis*, the West Virginia legislature amended its statutes to require all schools therein to conduct courses of instruction in history, civics, and in the Constitutions of the United States and of the State "for the purpose of teaching, fostering and perpetuating the ideals, principles and spirit of Americanism, and increasing the knowledge of the organization and machinery of the government." West Virginia's Board of Education was directed, with advice of the State Superintendent of Schools, to "prescribe the courses of study covering these subjects" for public schools. The Act made it the duty of private, parochial and denominational schools to prescribe courses of study "similar to those required for the public schools."

The Board of Education on January 9, 1942, adopted a resolution containing recitals taken largely from the Court's *Gobitis* opinion and ordering that the salute to the flag become "a regular part of the program of activities in the public schools," that all teachers and pupils "shall be required to participate in the salute honoring the Nation represented by the Flag; provided, however, that refusal to salute the Flag be regarded as an Act of insubordination, and shall be dealt with accordingly."

The resolution originally required the "commonly accepted salute to the Flag" which it defined. Objections to the salute as "being too much like Hitler's" were raised by the Parent and Teachers Association, the Boy and Girl Scouts, the Red Cross, and the Federation of Women's Clubs. Some modification appears to have been made in deference to these objections, but no concession was made to Jehovah's Witnesses. What is now required is the "stiff-arm" salute, the saluter to keep the right hand raised with palm turned up while the following is repeated: "I pledge allegiance to the Flag of the United States of America and to the Republic for which it stands; one Nation, indivisible, with liberty and justice for all."

Failure to conform is "insubordination" dealt with by expulsion. Readmission is denied by statute until compliance. Meanwhile the expelled child is "unlawfully absent" and may be proceeded against as a delinquent. His parents or guardians are liable to prosecution, and if convicted are subject to fine not exceeding $50 and jail term not exceeding thirty days.

Appellees, Walter Barnette, Paul Stull, and Lucy McClure, citizens of the United States and of West Virginia, brought suit in the United States District Court for themselves and others similarly situated, asking its injunction [court order to prohibit an act] to restrain enforcement of these laws and regulations against Jehovah's Witnesses. The Witnesses are an unincorporated body teaching that the obligation imposed by law of God is superior to that of laws enacted by temporal government. Their religious beliefs include a literal version of Exodus, Chapter 20, verses 4 and 5, which says: "Thou shalt not make unto thee any graven image, or any likeness of anything that is in heaven above, or that is in the earth beneath, or that is in the water under the earth; thou shalt not bow down thyself to them, nor serve them." They consider that the flag is an "image" within this command. For this reason they refuse to salute it.

Children of this faith have been expelled from school and are threatened with exclusion for no other cause. Officials threaten to send them to reformatories maintained for criminally inclined juveniles. Parents of such children have been prosecuted and are threatened with prosecutions for causing delinquency.

. . . . The cause was submitted . . . to a District Court of three judges. It restrained [halted] enforcement. . . . [T]he Board of Education . . . appeal[ed].

This case calls upon us to reconsider a precedent decision, as the Court throughout its history often has been required to do. Before turning to the *Gobitis* Case, however, it is desirable to notice certain characteristics by which this controversy is distinguished.

The freedom asserted by [Barnette, Stull, and McClure] does not bring them into collision with rights asserted by any other individual. It is such conflicts which most frequently require intervention of the State to determine where the rights of one end and those of another begin. But the refusal of these persons to participate in the ceremony does not interfere with or deny rights of others to do so. Nor is there any question in this case that their behavior is peaceable and orderly. The sole conflict is between authority and rights of the individual. The State asserts power to condition access to public education on making a prescribed sign and profession and at the same time to coerce attendance by punishing both parent and child. The latter stand on a right of self-determination in matters that touch individual opinion and personal attitude.

As the present Chief Justice [Harlan Fiske Stone] said in dissent in the *Gobitis* Case, the State may "require teaching by instruction and study of all in our history and in the structure and organization of our government, including the guaranties of civil liberty, which tend to inspire patriotism and love of country." Here, however, we are dealing with a compulsion of students to declare a belief. They are not merely made acquainted with the flag salute so that they may be informed as to what it is or even what it means. The issue here is whether this slow and easily neglected route to aroused loyalties constitutionally may be short-cut by substituting a compulsory salute and slogan. . . .

There is no doubt that, in connection with the pledges, the flag salute is a form of utterance. Symbolism is a primitive but effective way of communicating ideas. The use of an emblem or flag to symbolize some system, idea, institution, or personality, is a short cut from mind to mind. Causes and nations, political parties, lodges and ecclesiastical groups seek to knit the loyalty of their followings to a flag or banner, a color or design. The State announces rank, function, and authority through crowns and maces, uniforms and black robes; the church speaks through the Cross, the Crucifix, the altar and shrine, and clerical raiment. Symbols of State often convey political ideas just as religious symbols come to convey theological ones. Associated with many of these symbols are appropriate gestures of acceptance or respect: a salute, a bowed or bared head, a bended knee. A person gets from a symbol the meaning he puts into it, and what is one man's comfort and inspiration is another's jest and scorn.

Over a decade ago Chief Justice Hughes led this Court in holding that the display of a red flag as a symbol of opposition by peaceful and legal means to organized government was protected by the free speech guaranties of the Constitution. Here it is the State that employs a flag as a symbol of adherence to government as presently organized. It requires the individual to communicate by word and sign his acceptance of the political ideas it thus bespeaks. Objection to this form of communication when coerced is an old one, well known to the framers of the Bill of Rights.

It is also to be noted that the compulsory flag salute and pledge requires affirmation of a belief and an attitude of mind. It is not clear whether the regulation contemplates that pupils forego any contrary convictions of their own and become unwilling converts to the prescribed ceremony or whether it will be acceptable if they simulate assent by words without belief and by a gesture barren of meaning. It is now a commonplace that censorship or suppression of expression of opinion is tolerated by our Constitution only when the expression presents a clear and present danger of action of a kind the State is empowered to prevent and punish. It would seem that involuntary affirmation could be commanded only on even more immediate and urgent grounds than silence. But here the power of compulsion is invoked without any allegation that remaining passive during a flag salute ritual creates a clear and present danger that would justify an effort even to muffle expression. To sustain [uphold] the compulsory flag salute we are required to say that a Bill of Rights which guards the individual's right to speak his own mind, left it open to public authorities to compel him to utter what is not in his mind.

Whether the First Amendment to the Constitution will permit officials to order observance of ritual of this nature does not depend upon whether as a voluntary exercise we would think it to be good, bad or merely innocuous. Any credo of nationalism is likely to include what some disapprove or to omit what others think essential, and to give off different overtones as it takes on different accents or interpretations. If official power exists to coerce acceptance of any patriotic creed, what it shall contain cannot be decided by courts, but must be largely discretionary with the ordaining authority, whose power to prescribe would no doubt include power to amend. Hence validity of the asserted power to force an American citizen publicly to profess any statement of belief or to engage in any ceremony of assent to one, presents questions of power that must be considered independently of any idea we may have as to the utility of the ceremony in question.

Nor does the issue as we see it turn on one's possession of particular religious views or the sincerity with which they are held. While religion supplies [Barnette, Stull, and McClure's] motive for enduring the discomforts of making the issue in this case, many citizens who do not share these religious views hold such a compulsory rite to infringe constitutional liberty of the individual. It is not necessary to inquire whether nonconformist beliefs will exempt from the duty to salute unless we first find power to make the salute a legal duty.

The *Gobitis* decision, however, *assumed,* as did the argument in that case and in this, that power exists in the

State to impose the flag salute discipline upon school children in general. The Court only examined and rejected a claim based on religious beliefs of immunity from an unquestioned general rule. The question which underlies the flag salute controversy is whether such a ceremony so touching matters of opinion and political attitude may be imposed upon the individual by official authority under powers committed to any political organization under our Constitution. We examine rather than assume existence of this power and . . . re-examine specific grounds assigned for the *Gobitis* decision.

1. It was said that the flag-salute controversy confronted the Court with "the problem which Lincoln cast in memorable dilemma: 'Must a government of necessity be too *strong* for the liberties of its people, or too *weak* to maintain its own existence?'" and that the answer must be in favor of strength.

We think these issues may be examined free of pressure or restraint growing out of such considerations.

It may be doubted whether Mr. Lincoln would have thought that the strength of government to maintain itself would be impressively vindicated by our confirming power of the state to expel a handful of children from school. Such oversimplification, so handy in political debate, often lacks the precision necessary to postulates of judicial reasoning. If validly applied to this problem, the utterance cited would resolve every issue of power in favor of those in authority and would require us to override every liberty thought to weaken or delay execution of their policies.

Government of limited power need not be anemic government. Assurance that rights are secure tends to diminish fear and jealousy of strong government, and by making us feel safe to live under it makes for its better support. Without promise of a limiting Bill of Rights it is doubtful if our Constitution could have mustered enough strength to enable its ratification. To enforce those rights today is not to choose weak government over strong government. It is only to adhere as a means of strength to individual freedom of mind in preference to officially disciplined uniformity for which history indicates a disappointing and disastrous end.

The subject now before us exemplifies this principle. Free public education, if faithful to the ideal of secular instruction and political neutrality, will not be partisan or enemy of any class, creed, party, or faction. If it is to impose any ideological discipline, however, each party or denomination must seek to control, or failing that, to weaken the influence of the educational system. Observance of the limitations of the Constitution will not weaken government in the field appropriate for its exercise.

2. It was also considered in the *Gobitis* Case that functions of educational officers in states, counties and school districts were such that to interfere with their authority "would in effect make us the school board for the country."

The Fourteenth Amendment, as now applied to the States, protects the citizen against the State itself and all of its creatures - Boards of Education not excepted. These have, of course, important, delicate, and highly discretionary functions, but none that they may not perform within the limits of the Bill of Rights. That they are educating the young for citizenship is reason for scrupulous protection of Constitutional freedoms of the individual, if we are not to strangle the free mind at its source and teach youth to discount important principles of our government as mere platitudes.

Such Boards are numerous and their territorial jurisdiction often small. But small and local authority may feel less sense of responsibility to the Constitution, and agencies of publicity may be less vigilant in calling it to account. The action of Congress in making flag observance voluntary and respecting the conscience of the objector in a matter so vital as raising the Army contrasts sharply with these local regulations in matters relatively trivial to the welfare of the nation. There are village tyrants as well as village Hampdens, but none who acts under color of law is beyond reach of the Constitution.

3. The *Gobitis* opinion reasoned that this is a field "where courts possess no marked and certainly no controlling competence," that it is committed to the legislatures as well as the courts to guard cherished liberties and that it is constitutionally appropriate to "fight out the wise use of legislative authority in the forum of public opinion and before legislative assemblies rather than to transfer such a contest to the judicial arena," since all the "effective means of inducing political changes are left free."

The very purpose of a Bill of Rights was to withdraw certain subjects from the vicissitudes of political controversy, to place them beyond the reach of majorities and officials and to establish them as legal principles to be applied by the courts. One's right to life, liberty, and property, to free speech, a free press, freedom of worship and assembly, and other fundamental rights may not be submitted to vote; they depend on the outcome of no elections.

In weighing arguments of the parties it is important to distinguish between the due process clause of the Fourteenth Amendment as an instrument for transmitting the principles of the First Amendment and those cases in which it is applied for its own sake. The test of legislation which collides with the Fourteenth Amendment, because it also collides with the principles of the First, is much more definite than the test when only the Fourteenth is involved. Much of the vagueness of the due process clause disappears when the specific prohibitions of the First become its standard. The right of a State to regulate, for example, a public utility may well include, so far as the due process test is concerned, power to impose all of the restrictions which a legislature may have a "rational basis" for adopting. But freedoms of speech and of press, of assembly, and of worship may not be infringed on such slender grounds. They are susceptible of restriction only to prevent grave and immediate danger to interests which the state may lawfully protect. It is important to note that while it is the Fourteenth Amendment which bears directly upon the State it is the more specific limiting principles of the First Amendment that finally governs this case.

Nor does our duty to apply the Bill of Rights to assertions of official authority depend upon our possession of marked competence in the field where the invasion of rights occurs. True, the task of translating the majestic generalities of the Bill of Rights, conceived as part of the pattern of liberal government in the eighteenth century, into concrete restraints on officials dealing with the problems of the twentieth century, is one to disturb self-confidence. These principles grew in soil which also produced a philosophy that the individual was the center of society, that his liberty was attainable through mere absence of governmental restraints, and that government should be entrusted with few controls and only the mildest supervision over men's affairs. We must transplant these rights to a soil in which the laissez-faire concept or principle of non-interference has withered at least as to economic affairs, and social advancements are increasingly sought through closer integration of society and through expanded and strengthened governmental controls. These changed conditions often deprive precedents of reliability and cast us more than we would choose upon our own judgment. But we act in these matters not by authority of our competence but by force of our commissions. We cannot, because of modest estimates of our competence in such specialties as public education, withhold the judgment that history authenticates as the function of this Court when liberty is infringed.

4. Lastly, and this is the very heart of the *Gobitis* opinion, it reasons that "national unity is the basis of national security," that the authorities have "the right to select appropriate means for its attainment," and hence reaches the conclusion that such compulsory measures toward "national unity" are constitutional. Upon the verity of this assumption depends our answer in this case.

National unity as an end which officials may foster by persuasion and example is not in question. The problem is whether under our Constitution compulsion as here employed is a permissible means for its achievement.

Struggles to coerce uniformity of sentiment in support of
some end thought essential to their time and country have
been waged by many good as well as by evil men.
Nationalism is a relatively recent phenomenon but at
other times and places the ends have been racial or
territorial security, support of a dynasty or regime, and
particular plans for saving souls. As first and moderate
methods to attain unity have failed, those bent on its
accomplishment must resort to an ever increasing severity.
As governmental pressure toward unity becomes greater,
so strife becomes more bitter as to whose unity it shall be.
Probably no deeper division of our people could proceed
from any provocation than from finding it necessary to
choose what doctrine and whose program public
educational officials shall compel youth to unite in
embracing. Ultimate futility of such attempts to compel
coherence is the lesson of every such effort from the
Roman drive to stamp out Christianity as a disturber of
its pagan unity, the Inquisition, as a means to religious and
dynastic unity, the Siberian exiles as a means to Russian
unity, down to the fast failing efforts of our present
totalitarian enemies.   Those who begin coercive
elimination of dissent soon find themselves exterminating
dissenters. Compulsory unification of opinion achieves
only the unanimity of the graveyard.

It seems trite but necessary to say that the First
Amendment to our Constitution was designed to avoid
these ends by avoiding these beginnings. There is no
mysticism in the American concept of the State or of the
nature or origin of its authority. We set up government
by consent of the governed, and the Bill of Rights denies
those in power any legal opportunity to coerce that
consent. Authority here is to be controlled by public
opinion, not public opinion by authority.

The case is made difficult not because the principles of its decision are obscure but because the flag involved is our own. Nevertheless, we apply the limitations of the Constitution with no fear that freedom to be intellectually and spiritually diverse or even contrary will disintegrate the social organization. To believe that patriotism will not flourish if patriotic ceremonies are voluntary and spontaneous instead of a compulsory routine is to make an unflattering estimate of the appeal of our institutions to free minds. We can have intellectual individualism and the rich cultural diversities that we owe to exceptional minds only at the price of occasional eccentricity and abnormal attitudes. When they are so harmless to others or to the State as those we deal with here, the price is not too great. But freedom to differ is not limited to things that do not matter much. That would be a mere shadow of freedom. The test of its substance is the right to differ as to things that touch the heart of the existing order.

If there is any fixed star in our constitutional constellation, it is that no official, high or petty, can prescribe what shall be orthodox in politics, nationalism, religion, or other matters of opinion or force citizens to confess by word or act their faith therein. If there are any circumstances which permit an exception, they do not now occur to us.

We think the action of the local authorities in compelling the flag salute and pledge transcends constitutional limitations on their power and invades the sphere of intellect and spirit which it is the purpose of the First Amendment to our Constitution to reserve from all official control.

The decision of this Court in *Minersville School District v. Gobitis* and the holdings of those few per curiam [by the whole court, without one author] decisions which preceded and foreshadowed it are overruled, and the judgment enjoining [halting] enforcement of the West Virginia Regulation is affirmed [upheld].

ILLEGAL SEARCH & SEIZURE

MAPP v. OHIO

The United States Supreme Court ruled in 1949 that evidence obtained by police in an illegal search and seizure was inadmissible in a *federal* court.

On May 23, 1957 three Cleveland police officers arrived at the door of Dorlee Mapp's home and demanded admittance without explanation. Mapp refused to admit them without a search warrant.

Later that day seven police officers forced their way into Mapp's home. Mapp again demanded to see a search warrant. A struggle erupted between Mapp and the police over a supposed search warrant. Mapp was subdued, handcuffed, and held prisoner in her home while the police conducted a room-by-room search. During the search, later described as a ransacking, the police discovered "obscene materials." Mapp was then arrested and charged under a state obscenity statute.

Dorlee Mapp was tried for possession of obscene materials in Ohio Common Pleas Court. No search warrant was ever produced. The "obscene materials" obtained by illegal search and seizure were admitted into evidence and Mapp was found guilty. The Ohio Court of Appeals and the Ohio Supreme Court upheld her conviction. The penalty was imprisonment for no more than one and no less than seven years. Mapp appealed to the U.S. Supreme Court claiming that evidence obtained by the police in an illegal search and seizure, inadmissible in a *federal court*, should not be admissible in a *state court* either.

Oral arguments were heard before the Court March 20, 1961 and a decision was announced June 19, 1961 by Associate Justice Thomas Clark.

The complete text of *Mapp v. Ohio* can be found in volume 367 of *United State Reports.*

MAPP v. OHIO

JUNE 19, 1961

JUSTICE THOMAS CLARK delivered the opinion of the Court: Appellant [Dorlee Mapp] stands convicted of knowingly having had in her possession and under her control certain lewd and lascivious books, pictures, and photographs in violation of . . . Ohio's Revised Code. . . . [T]he Supreme Court of Ohio found that her conviction was valid though "based primarily upon the introduction in evidence of lewd and lascivious books and pictures unlawfully seized during an unlawful search of defendant's home. . . ."

On May 23, 1957, three Cleveland police officers arrived at [Mapp's] residence in that city pursuant to information that "a person [was] hiding out in the home, who was wanted for questioning in connection with a recent bombing, and that there was a large amount of policy [gambling] paraphernalia being hidden in the home." Miss Mapp and her daughter by a former marriage lived on the top floor of the two-family dwelling. Upon their arrival at that house, the officers knocked on the door and demanded entrance but [Mapp], after telephoning her attorney, refused to admit them without a search warrant. They advised their headquarters of the situation and undertook a surveillance of the house.

The officers again sought entrance some three hours later when four or more additional officers arrived on the scene. When Miss Mapp did not come to the door immediately, at least one of the several doors to the house was forcibly opened and the policemen gained admittance.

Meanwhile Miss Mapp's attorney arrived, but the officers,
having secured their own entry, and continuing in their
defiance of the law, would permit him neither to see Miss
Mapp nor to enter the house. It appears that Miss Mapp
was halfway down the stairs from the upper floor to the
front door when the officers, in this highhanded manner,
broke into the hall. She demanded to see the search
warrant. A paper, claimed to be a warrant, was held up
by one of the officers. She grabbed the "warrant" and
placed it in her bosom. A struggle ensued in which the
officers recovered the piece of paper and as a result of
which they handcuffed [Mapp] because she had been
"belligerent" in resisting their official rescue of the
"warrant" from her person. Running roughshod over
[Mapp], a policeman "grabbed" her, "twisted [her] hand,"
and she "yelled [and] pleaded with him" because "it was
hurting." [Mapp], in handcuffs, was then forcibly taken
upstairs to her bedroom where the officers searched a
dresser, a chest of drawers, a closet and some suitcases.
They also looked into a photo album and through personal
papers belonging to [Mapp]. The search spread to the rest
of the second floor including the child's bedroom, the
living room, the kitchen and a dinette. The basement of
the building and a trunk found therein were also searched.
The obscene materials for possession of which she was
ultimately convicted were discovered in the course of that
widespread search.

At the trial no search warrant was produced by the
prosecution, nor was the failure to produce one explained
or accounted for. At best, "There is, in the record,
considerable doubt as to whether there ever was any
warrant for the search of [Mapp]'s home." The Ohio
Supreme Court believed a "reasonable argument" could be
made that the conviction should be reversed "because the

'methods' employed to obtain the [evidence] . . . were such as to 'offend a sense of justice,'" but the court found determinative the fact that the evidence had not been taken "from [Mapp]'s person by the use of brutal or offensive physical force against [her]."

The State says that even if the search were made without authority, or otherwise unreasonably, it is not prevented from using the unconstitutionally seized evidence at trial, citing *Wolf v. Colorado*, in which this Court did indeed hold "that in a prosecution in a State court for a State crime the Fourteenth Amendment does not forbid the admission of evidence obtained by an unreasonable search and seizure." On this appeal . . . it is urged once again that we review that holding.

Seventy-five years ago, in *Boyd v. United States*, considering the Fourth and Fifth Amendments as running "almost into each other" on the facts before it, this Court held that the doctrines of those Amendments

> "apply to all invasions on the part of the government and its employes of the sanctity of a man's home and the privacies of life. It is not the breaking of his doors, and the rummaging of his drawers, that constitutes the essence of the offence; but it is the invasion of his indefeasible right of personal security, personal liberty and private property. . . . Breaking into a house and opening boxes and drawers are circumstances of aggravation; but any forcible and compulsory extortion of a man's own testimony or of his private papers to be used as evidence to convict him of crime or to forfeit his goods, is within the condemnation . . . [of those Amendments]."

The Court noted that

> "constitutional provisions for the security of
> person and property should be liberally
> construed. . . . It is the duty of courts to be
> watchful for the constitutional rights of the
> citizen, and against any stealthy encroachments
> thereon."

In this jealous regard for maintaining the integrity of
individual rights, the Court gave life to Madison's
prediction that "independent tribunals of justice . . . will
be naturally led to resist every encroachment upon rights
expressly stipulated for in the Constitution by the
declaration of rights." Concluding, the Court specifically
referred to the use of the evidence there seized as
"unconstitutional."

Less than 30 years after *Boyd*, this Court, in *Weeks v.
United States*, stated that

> "the Fourth Amendment . . . put the courts of the
> United States and Federal officials, in the
> exercise of their power and authority, under
> limitations and restraints [and] . . . forever
> secure[d] the people, their persons, houses, papers
> and effects against all unreasonable searches and
> seizures under the guise of law . . . and the duty
> of giving to it force and effect is obligatory upon
> all entrusted under our Federal system with the
> enforcement of the laws."

Specifically dealing with the use of the evidence
unconstitutionally seized, the Court concluded:

"If letters and private documents can thus be
seized and held and used in evidence against a
citizen accused of an offense, the protection of
the Fourth Amendment declaring his right to be
secure against such searches and seizures is of no
value, and, so far as those thus placed are
concerned, might as well be stricken from the
Constitution. The efforts of the courts and their
officials to bring the guilty to punishment,
praiseworthy as they are, are not to be aided by
the sacrifice of those great principles established
by years of endeavor and suffering which have
resulted in their embodiment in the fundamental
law of the land."

Finally, the Court in that case clearly stated that use of
the seized evidence involved "a denial of the
constitutional rights of the accused." Thus, in the year
1914, in the *Weeks* case, this Court "for the first time"
held that "in a federal prosecution the Fourth Amendment
barred the use of evidence secured through an illegal
search and seizure." This Court has ever since required of
federal law officers a strict adherence to that command
which this Court has held to be a clear, specific, and
constitutionally required - even if judicially implied -
deterrent safeguard without insistence upon which the
Fourth Amendment would have been reduced to "a form
of words." It meant, quite simply, that "conviction by
means of unlawful seizures and enforced confessions . . .
should find no sanction in the judgments of the courts
. . . ," and that such evidence "shall not be used at all."

. . . . In *Byars v. United States,* a unanimous Court
declared that "the doctrine [cannot] . . . be tolerated *under
our constitutional system,* that evidences of crime

discovered by a federal officer in making a search without lawful warrant may be used against the victim of the unlawful search where a timely challenge has been interposed." The Court, in *Olmstead v. United States*, in unmistakable language restated the *Weeks* rule:

"The striking outcome of the *Weeks* case and those which followed it was the sweeping declaration that the Fourth Amendment, although not referring to or limiting the use of evidence in courts, really forbade its introduction if obtained by government officers through a violation of the Amendment."

In *McNabb v. United States*, we note this statement:

"[A] conviction in the federal courts, the foundation of which is evidence obtained in disregard of liberties deemed fundamental by the Constitution, cannot stand. And this Court has, on Constitutional grounds, set aside convictions, both in the federal and state courts, which were based upon confessions 'secured by protracted and repeated questioning of ignorant and untutored persons, in whose minds the power of officers was greatly magnified' . . . or 'who have been unlawfully held incommunicado without advice of friends or counsel'. . . ."

. . . . In 1949, 35 years after *Weeks* was announced, this Court in *Wolf v. Colorado*, again for the first time, discussed the effect of the Fourth Amendment upon the States through the operation of the Due Process Clause of the Fourteenth Amendment. It said:

"[W]e have no hesitation in saying that were a
State affirmatively to sanction such police
incursion into privacy it would run counter to the
guaranty of the Fourteenth Amendment."

Nevertheless, after declaring that the "security of one's
privacy against arbitrary intrusion by the police" is
"implicit in 'the concept of ordered liberty' and as such
enforceable against the States through the Due Process
Clause," and announcing that it "stoutly adhere[d]" to the
Weeks decision, the Court decided that the *Weeks*
exclusionary rule would not then be imposed upon the
States as "an essential ingredient of the right."   The
Court's reasons for not considering essential to the right
to privacy, as a curb imposed upon the States by the Due
Process Clause, that which decades before had been
posited as part and parcel of the Fourth Amendment's
limitation upon federal encroachment of individual
privacy, were bottomed on factual considerations.

. . . . [W]e will consider the current validity of the factual
grounds upon which *Wolf* was based.

The Court in *Wolf* first stated that "[t]he contrariety of
views of the States" on the adoption of the exclusionary
rule of *Weeks* was "particularly impressive"; and, in this
connection, that it could not "brush aside the experience
of States which deem the incidence of such conduct by
the police too slight to call for a deterrent remedy . . . by
overriding the [States'] relevant rules of evidence."   While
in 1949, prior to the *Wolf* case, almost two-thirds of the
States were opposed to the use of the exclusionary rule,
now, despite the *Wolf* case, more than half of those since
passing upon it, by their own legislative or judicial
decision, have wholly or partly adopted or adhered to the

Weeks rule. Significantly, among those now following the rule is California, which, according to its highest court, was "compelled to reach that conclusion because other remedies have completely failed to secure compliance with the constitutional provisions. . . ." In connection with this California case [*People v. Cahan*], we note that the second basis elaborated in *Wolf* in support of its failure to enforce the exclusionary doctrine against the States was that "other means of protection" have been afforded "the right to privacy." The experience of California that such other remedies have been worthless and futile is buttressed by the experience of other States. The obvious futility of relegating the Fourth Amendment to the protection of other remedies has, moreover, been recognized by this Court since *Wolf.*

Likewise, time has set its face against what *Wolf* called the "weighty testimony" of *People v. Defore.* There Justice (then Judge) Cardozo, rejecting adoption of the *Weeks* exclusionary rule in New York, had said that "[t]he Federal rule as it stands is either too strict or too lax." However, the force of that reasoning has been largely vitiated by later decisions of this Court. These include the recent discarding of the "silver platter" doctrine which allowed federal judicial use of evidence seized in violation of the Constitution by state agents; the relaxation of the formerly strict requirements as to standing to challenge the use of evidence thus seized, so that now the procedure of exclusion, "ultimately referable to constitutional safeguards," is available to anyone even "legitimately on [the] premises" unlawfully searched; and, finally, the formulation of a method to prevent state use of evidence unconstitutionally seized by federal agents. Because there can be no fixed formula, we are admittedly met with "recurring questions of the reasonableness of searches," but less is not to be expected when dealing with a Constitution, and, at any rate, "[r]easonableness is in the first instance for the [trial court] . . . to determine."

It, therefore, plainly appears that the factual considerations supporting the failure of the *Wolf* Court to include the *Weeks* exclusionary rule when it recognized the enforceability of the right to privacy against the States in 1949, while not basically relevant to the constitutional consideration, could not, in any analysis, now be deemed controlling.

Some five years after *Wolf*, in answer to a plea made here Term after Term that we overturn its doctrine on applicability of the *Weeks* exclusionary rule, this Court indicated that such should not be done until the States had "adequate opportunity to adopt or reject the [*Weeks*] rule."

. . . . And only last Term, after again carefully re-examining the *Wolf* doctrine in *Elkins v. United States*, the Court pointed out that "the controlling principles" as to search and seizure and the problem of admissibility "seemed clear" until the announcement in *Wolf* "that the Due Process Clause of the Fourteenth Amendment does not itself require state courts to adopt the exclusionary rule" of the *Weeks* case. At the same time, the Court pointed out, "the underlying constitutional doctrine which *Wolf* established . . . that the Federal Constitution . . . prohibits unreasonable searches and seizures by state officers" had undermined the "foundation upon which the admissibility of state-seized evidence in a federal trial originally rested. . . ." The Court concluded that it was therefore obliged to hold . . . that all evidence obtained by an unconstitutional search and seizure was inadmissible in

a federal court regardless of its source. Today we once
again examine *Wolf*'s constitutional documentation of the
right to privacy free from unreasonable state intrusion,
and, after its dozen years on our books, are led by it to
close the only courtroom door remaining open to evidence
secured by official lawlessness in flagrant abuse of that
basic right, reserved to all persons as a specific guarantee
against that very same unlawful conduct. We hold that all
evidence obtained by searches and seizures in violation of
the Constitution is, by that same authority, inadmissible in
a state court.

Since the Fourteenth Amendment's right of privacy has
been declared enforceable against the States through the
Due Process Clause of the Fourteenth, it is enforceable
against them by the same sanction of exclusion as is used
against the Federal Government. Were it otherwise, then
just as without the *Weeks* rule the assurance against
unreasonable federal searches and seizures would be "a
form of words," . . . so too, without that rule the freedom
from state invasions of privacy would be so ephemeral . . .
as not to merit this Court's high regard as a freedom
"implicit in the concept of ordered liberty." At the time
that the Court held in *Wolf* that the Amendment was
applicable to the States through the Due Process Clause,
the cases of this Court, as we have seen, had steadfastly
held that as to federal officers the Fourth Amendment
included the exclusion of the evidence seized in violation
of its provisions. Even *Wolf* "stoutly adhered" to that
proposition. . . . [I]n extending the substantive [essential]
protections of due process to all constitutionally
unreasonable searches - state or federal - it was logically
and constitutionally necessary that the exclusion doctrine
- an essential part of the right to privacy - be also insisted
upon as an essential ingredient of the right newly

recognized by the *Wolf* case. In short, the admission of the new constitutional right by *Wolf* could not consistently tolerate denial of its most important constitutional privilege, namely, the exclusion of the evidence which an accused had been forced to give by reason of the unlawful seizure. To hold otherwise is to grant the right but in reality to withhold its privilege and enjoyment. Only last year the Court itself recognized that the purpose of the exclusionary rule "is to deter - to compel respect for the constitutional guaranty in the only effectively available way - by removing the incentive to disregard it."

Indeed, we are aware of no restraint . . . conditioning the enforcement of any other basic constitutional right. The right to privacy, no less important than any other right carefully and particularly reserved to the people, would stand in marked contrast to all other rights declared as "basic to a free society." This Court has not hesitated to enforce as strictly against the States as it does against the Federal Government the rights of free speech and of a free press, the rights to notice and to a fair, public trial, including, as it does, the right not to be convicted by use of a coerced confession, however logically relevant it be, and without regard to its reliability. And nothing could be more certain than that when a coerced confession is involved, "the relevant rules of evidence" are overridden without regard to "the incidence of such conduct by the police," slight or frequent. Why should not the same rule apply to what is tantamount to coerced testimony by way of unconstitutional seizure of goods, papers, effects, documents, etc.? We find that, as to the Federal Government, the Fourth and Fifth Amendments and, as to the States, the freedom from unconscionable invasions of privacy and the freedom from convictions based upon coerced confessions do enjoy an "intimate relation" in their perpetuation of "principles of humanity and civil liberty [secured] . . . only after years of struggle." They express "supplementing phases of the same constitutional purpose - to maintain inviolate large areas of personal privacy." The philosophy of each Amendment and of each freedom is complementary to, although not dependent upon, that of the other in its sphere of influence - the very least that together they assure in either sphere is that no man is to be convicted on unconstitutional evidence.

Moreover, our holding that the exclusionary rule is an essential part of both the Fourth and Fourteenth Amendments is not only the logical dictate of prior cases, but it also makes very good sense. There is no war between the Constitution and common sense. Presently, a federal prosecutor may make no use of evidence illegally seized, but a State's attorney across the street may, although he supposedly is operating under the enforceable prohibitions of the same Amendment. Thus the State, by admitting evidence unlawfully seized, serves to encourage disobedience to the Federal Constitution which it is bound to uphold. . . . Yet the double standard recognized until today hardly put such a thesis into practice. In non-exclusionary States, federal officers, being human, were by it invited to and did . . . step across the street to the State's attorney with their unconstitutionally seized evidence. Prosecution on the basis of that evidence was then had in a state court in utter disregard of the enforceable Fourth Amendment. If the fruits of an unconstitutional search had been inadmissible in both state and federal courts, this inducement to evasion would have been sooner eliminated. . . .

Federal-state cooperation in the solution of crime under constitutional standards will be promoted, if only by recognition of their now mutual obligation to respect the same fundamental criteria in their approaches. . . . Denying shortcuts to only one of two cooperating law enforcement agencies tends naturally to breed legitimate suspicion of "working arrangements" whose results are equally tainted.

There are those who say, as did Justice (then Judge) Cardozo, that under our constitutional exclusionary doctrine "[t]he criminal is to go free because the constable has blundered." In some cases this will undoubtedly be the result. But, as was said in *Elkins*, "there is another consideration - the imperative of judicial integrity." The criminal goes free, if he must, but it is the law that sets him free. Nothing can destroy a government more quickly than its failure to observe its own laws, or worse, its disregard of the charter of its own existence. As Justice Brandeis, dissenting, said in *Olmstead v. United States*, "Our Government is the potent, the omnipresent teacher. For good or for ill, it teaches the whole people by its example. . . . If the Government becomes a lawbreaker, it breeds contempt for law; it invites every man to become a law unto himself; it invites anarchy." Nor can it lightly be assumed that, as a practical matter, adoption of the exclusionary rule fetters law enforcement. Only last year this Court expressly considered that contention and found that "pragmatic evidence of a sort" to the contrary was not wanting. The Court noted that

"The federal courts themselves have operated under the exclusionary rule of *Weeks* for almost half a century; yet it has not been suggested either that the Federal Bureau of Investigation has thereby been rendered ineffective, or that the administration of criminal justice in the federal courts has thereby been disrupted. Moreover, the experience of the states is impressive. . . . The movement towards the rule of exclusion has been halting but seemingly inexorable."

The ignoble shortcut to conviction left open to the State tends to destroy the entire system of constitutional restraints on which the liberties of the people rest. Having once recognized that the right to privacy embodied in the Fourth Amendment is enforceable against the States, and that the right to be secure against rude invasions of privacy by state officers is, therefore, constitutional in origin, we can no longer permit that right to remain an empty promise. Because it is enforceable in the same manner and to like effect as other basic rights secured by the Due Process Clause, we can no longer permit it to be revocable at the whim of any police officer who, in the name of law enforcement itself, chooses to suspend its enjoyment. Our decision, founded on reason and truth, gives to the individual no more than that which the Constitution guarantees him, to the police officer no less than that to which honest law enforcement is entitled, and, to the courts, that judicial integrity so necessary in the true administration of justice.

The judgment of the Supreme Court of Ohio is reversed and the cause remanded [sent back to the lower court] for further proceedings not inconsistent with this opinion.

INTERRACIAL MARRIAGE

LOVING v. VIRGINIA

The Commonwealth of Virginia adopted in 1924 the Racial Integrity Act, an antimiscegenation law prohibiting and punishing interracial marriage between "white persons" and "colored persons."

In January 1959 two Virginia citizens, Richard Perry Loving, a white male, and his wife, Mildred Jeter Loving, a black female, married six months before in the District of Columbia, pled guilty in a Caroline County, Virginia Circuit Court to violating the state's prohibition against interracial marriage. The punishment for miscegenation, a felony, was "confinement in the penitentiary for not less than one nor more than five years." The Lovings were each sentenced to one year in jail, which the judge then suspended on the condition that the Lovings leave Virginia and not return together for twenty-five years.

In November 1963 the Lovings, then residents of the District of Columbia, asked a Virginia trial court to throw out the guilty judgments and set aside their sentences on the grounds that Virginia's Racial Integrity Act violated their rights under the Fourteenth Amendment to the U.S. Constitution. The trial court denied their request in January 1965 and the Lovings appealed to Virginia's highest court, the Supreme Court of Appeals. On March 7, 1966 the Virginia Supreme Court of Appeals upheld the constitutionality of the anti-interracial law and affirmed the convictions. The Lovings appealed to the United States Supreme Court, which agreed to a review on December 12, 1966.

Oral arguments were heard before the Court on April 10, 1967 and a decision was announced June 12, 1967 by Chief Justice Earl Warren.

The complete text of *Loving v. Virginia* can be found in volume 388 of *United States Reports.*

LOVING v. VIRGINIA

JUNE 12, 1967

CHIEF JUSTICE EARL WARREN delivered the opinion of the Court: This case presents a constitutional question never addressed by this Court: whether a statutory scheme adopted by the State of Virginia to prevent marriages between persons solely on the basis of racial classifications violates the Equal Protection and Due Process Clauses of the Fourteenth Amendment. For reasons which seem to us to reflect the central meaning of those constitutional commands, we conclude that these statutes cannot stand consistently with the Fourteenth Amendment.

In June 1958, two residents of Virginia, Mildred Jeter, a Negro woman, and Richard Loving, a white man, were married in the District of Columbia pursuant to its laws. Shortly after their marriage, the Lovings returned to Virginia and established their marital abode in Caroline County. At the October Term, 1958, the Circuit Court of Caroline County, a grand jury issued an indictment charging the Lovings with violating Virginia's ban on interracial marriages. On January 6, 1959, the Lovings pleaded guilty to the charge and were sentenced to one year in jail; however, the trial judge suspended the sentence for a period of 25 years on the condition that the Lovings leave the State and not return to Virginia together for 25 years. He stated in an opinion that:

"Almighty God created the races white, black, yellow, malay and red, and he placed them on separate continents. And but for the interference with his arrangement there would be no cause for such marriages. The fact that he separated the races shows that he did not intend for the races to mix."

After their convictions, the Lovings took up residence in the District of Columbia. On November 6, 1963, they filed a motion [a request for a ruling] in the state trial court to vacate [throw out] the judgment and set aside the sentence on the ground that the statutes which they had violated were repugnant to the Fourteenth Amendment. The motion not having been decided by October 28, 1964, the Lovings instituted a class action [suit by a group of people with similar characteristics] in the United States District Court for the Eastern District of Virginia requesting that a three-judge court be convened to declare the Virginia antimiscegenation statutes unconstitutional and to enjoin [stop] state officials from enforcing their convictions. On January 22, 1965, the state trial judge denied the motion to [throw out] the sentences, and the Lovings [appealed] to the Supreme Court of Appeals of Virginia. On February 11, 1965, the three-judge District Court continued [postponed] the case to allow the Lovings to present their constitutional claims to the highest state court.

The Supreme Court of Appeals upheld the constitutionality of the antimiscegenation statutes and, after modifying the sentence, affirmed [upheld] the convictions. The Lovings appealed this decision, and we [agreed to hear the case].

The two statutes under which [the Lovings] were convicted and sentenced are part of a comprehensive statutory scheme aimed at prohibiting and punishing interracial marriages. The Lovings were convicted of violating Section 20-58 of the Virginia Code:

> "*Leaving State to evade law.* If any white person and colored person shall go out of this State, for the purpose of being married, and with the intention of returning, and be married out of it, and afterwards return to and reside in it, cohabiting as man and wife, they shall be punished as provided in Section 20-59, and the marriage shall be governed by the same law as if it had been solemnized in this State. The fact of their cohabitation here as man and wife shall be evidence of their marriage."

Section 20-59, which defines the penalty for miscegenation, provides:

> "*Punishment for marriage.* If any white person intermarry with a colored person, or any colored person intermarry with a white person, he shall be guilty of a felony and shall be punished by confinement in the penitentiary for not less than one nor more than five years."

Other central provisions in the Virginia statutory scheme are Section 20-57, which automatically voids all marriages between "a white person and a colored person" without any judicial proceeding, and Sections 20-54 and 1-14 which, respectively, define "white persons" and "colored persons and Indians" for purposes of the statutory prohibitions. The Lovings have never disputed in the course of this litigation that Mrs. Loving is a "colored person" or that Mr. Loving is a "white person" within the meanings given those terms by the Virginia Statutes.

Virginia is now one of 16 States which prohibit and
punish marriages on the basis of racial classifications.
Penalties for miscegenation arose as an incident to slavery
and have been common in Virginia since the colonial
period. The present statutory scheme dates from the
adoption of the Racial Integrity Act of 1924, passed
during the period of extreme nativism which followed the
end of the First World War. The central features of this
Act, and current Virginia law, are the absolute prohibition
of a "white person" marrying other than another "white
person," a prohibition against issuing marriage licenses
until the issuing official is satisfied that the applicants'
statements as to their race are correct, certificates of
"racial composition" to be kept by both local and state
registrars, and the carrying forward of earlier prohibitions
against racial intermarriage.

In upholding the constitutionality of these provisions in
the decision [of the court] below, the Supreme Court of
Appeals of Virginia referred to its 1955 decision in *Naim
v. Naim.* . . . In *Naim,* the state court concluded that the
State's legitimate purposes were "to preserve the racial
integrity of its citizens," and to prevent "the corruption of
blood," "a mongrel breed of citizens," and "the obliteration
of racial pride," obviously an endorsement of the doctrine
of White Supremacy. The court also reasoned that
marriage has traditionally been subject to state regulation
without federal intervention, and, consequently, the
regulation of marriage should be left to exclusive state
control by the Tenth Amendment.

While the state court is no doubt correct in asserting that
marriage is a social relation subject to the State's police
power, the State does not contend in its argument before
this Court that its powers to regulate marriage are

unlimited notwithstanding the commands of the Fourteenth Amendment. . . . Instead, the State argues that the meaning of the Equal Protection Clause, as illuminated by the statements of the Framers, is only that state penal laws containing an interracial element as part of the definition of the offense must apply equally to whites and Negroes in the sense that members of each race are punished to the same degree. Thus, the State contends that, because its miscegenation statutes punish equally both the white and the Negro participants in an interracial marriage, these statutes, despite their reliance on racial classifications, do not constitute an invidious discrimination based upon race. The second argument advanced by the State . . . is that, if the Equal Protection Clause does not outlaw miscegenation statutes because of their reliance on racial classifications, the question of constitutionality would thus become whether there was any rational basis for a State to treat interracial marriages differently from other marriages. On this question, the State argues, the scientific evidence is substantially in doubt and, consequently, this Court should defer to the wisdom of the state legislature in adopting its policy of discouraging interracial marriages.

Because we reject the notion that the mere "equal application" of a statute containing racial classifications is enough to remove the classifications from the Fourteenth Amendment's proscription of all invidious racial discriminations, we do not accept the State's contention that these statutes should be upheld if there is any possible basis for concluding that they serve a rational purpose. The mere fact of equal application does not mean that our analysis of these statutes should follow the approach we have taken in cases involving no racial discrimination where the Equal Protection Clause has been arrayed against a statute discriminating between the kinds of advertising which may be displayed on trucks in New York City, or an exemption in Ohio's ad valorem tax for merchandise owned by a nonresident in a storage warehouse. In these cases, involving distinctions not drawn according to race, the Court has merely asked whether there is any rational foundation for the discriminations, and has deferred to the wisdom of the state legislatures. In [this case], however, we deal with statutes containing racial classifications, and the fact of equal application does not immunize the statute from the very heavy burden of justification which the Fourteenth Amendment has traditionally required of state statutes drawn according to race.

The State argues that statements in the Thirty-ninth congress about the time of the passage of the Fourteenth Amendment indicate that the Framers did not intend the Amendment to make unconstitutional state miscegenation laws. Many of the statements alluded to by the State concern the debates over the Freedman's Bureau Bill, which President [Andrew] Johnson vetoed, and the Civil Rights Act of 1866, enacted over his veto. While these statements have some relevance to the intention of Congress in submitting the Fourteenth Amendment, it must be understood that they pertained to the passage of specific statutes and not to the broader, organic purpose of a constitutional amendment. As for the various statements directly concerning the Fourteenth Amendment, we have said in connection with a related problem, that although these historical sources "cast some light" they are not sufficient to resolve the problem; "[a]t best, they are inconclusive. The most avid proponents of the post-War Amendments undoubtedly intended them to remove all legal distinctions among 'all persons born or naturalized in the United States.' Their opponents, just as certainly, were antagonistic to both the letter and the spirit of the Amendments and wished them to have the most limited effect." We have rejected the proposition that the debates in the Thirty-ninth congress or in the state legislatures which ratified the Fourteenth Amendment supported the theory advanced by the State, that the requirement of equal protection of the laws is satisfied by penal laws defining offenses based on racial classifications so long as white and Negro participants in the offense were similarly punished.

The State finds support for its "equal application" theory in the decision of the Court in *Pace v. Alabama.* In that case, the Court upheld a conviction under an Alabama statute forbidding adultery or fornication between a white person and a Negro which imposed a greater penalty than that of a statute proscribing similar conduct by members of the same race. The Court reasoned that the statute could not be said to discriminate against Negroes because the punishment for each participant in the offense was the same. However, as recently as the 1964 Term, in rejecting the reasoning of that case, we stated "*Pace* represents a limited view of the Equal Protection Clause which has not withstood analysis in the subsequent decisions of this Court." As we there demonstrated, the Equal Protection Clause requires the consideration of whether the classifications drawn by any statute constitute an arbitrary and invidious discrimination. The clear and central purpose of the Fourteenth Amendment was to eliminate all official state sources of invidious racial discrimination in the States.

There can be no question but that Virginia's miscegenation statutes rest solely upon distinctions drawn

according to race. The statutes proscribe generally
accepted conduct if engaged in by members of different
races. Over the years, this Court has consistently
repudiated "[d]istinctions between citizens solely because
of their ancestry" as being "odious to a free people whose
institutions are founded upon the doctrine of equality."
At the very least, the Equal Protection Clause demands
that racial classifications, especially suspect in criminal
statutes, be subjected to the "most rigid scrutiny," and, if
they are ever to be upheld, they must be shown to be
necessary to the accomplishment of some permissible state
objective, independent of the racial discrimination which
it was the object of the Fourteenth Amendment to
eliminate. Indeed, two members of this Court have
already stated that they "cannot conceive of a valid
legislative purpose . . . which makes the color of a
person's skin the test of whether his conduct is a criminal
offense."

There is patently no legitimate overriding purpose
independent of invidious racial discrimination which
justifies this classification. The fact that Virginia
prohibits only interracial marriages involving white
persons demonstrates that the racial classifications must
stand on their own justification, as measures designed to
maintain White Supremacy. We have consistently denied
the constitutionality of measures which restrict the rights
of citizens on account of race. There can be no doubt that
restricting the freedom to marry solely because of racial
classifications violates the central meaning of the Equal
Protection Clause.

These statutes also deprive the Lovings of liberty without
due process of law in violation of the Due Process Clause

of the Fourteenth Amendment. The freedom to marry has long been recognized as one of the vital personal rights essential to the orderly pursuit of happiness by free men.

Marriage is one of the "basic civil rights of man," fundamental to our very existence and survival. To deny this fundamental freedom on so unsupportable a basis as the racial classifications embodied in these statutes, classifications so directly subversive of the principle of equality at the heart of the Fourteenth Amendment, is surely to deprive all the State's citizens of liberty without due process of law. The Fourteenth Amendment requires that the freedom of choice to marry not be restricted by invidious racial discriminations. Under our Constitution, the freedom to marry, or not marry, a person of another race resides with the individual and cannot be infringed by the State.

These convictions must be reversed.

It is so ordered.

MONKEY TRIALS

EPPERSON v. ARKANSAS

In 1928 Arkansas, joining Tennessee, Mississippi, Oklahoma, Florida, and Texas, passed a "monkey law," making it illegal to teach in their public schools man's evolution from apes. This theory of evolution originated in Charles Darwin's *On The Origin of Species* (1859). Any Arkansas teacher found guilty of teaching "evolution" or "Darwinism" would be fined and dismissed.

Prior to the beginning of the 1965-1966 school year, the official Arkansas textbook for high school biology, in compliance with the 1928 "monkey law," did not cover evolution. In September 1965 a new biology text, including evolution, was adopted for use by the Little Rock, Arkansas school system.

Susan Epperson was a 10th grade biology teacher at Little Rock's Central High School. Epperson, who held a master's degree in zoology from the University of Illinois, had been hired by the Little Rock school system in the fall of 1964. The adoption of the new evolution-inclusive textbook placed Epperson in an impossible legal situation. The State would dismiss her for teaching evolution. The School System would dismiss her for refusing to use the new textbook. Epperson asked the Arkansas Courts to protect her from the State and the School System.

The Chancellery Court found the statute unconstitutional, a violation of the First and Fourteenth Amendments. On appeal the Supreme Court of Arkansas reversed the lower court. Epperson appealed to the U.S. Supreme Court.

Oral arguments were heard by the Court on October 16, 1968 and a decision was announced on November 12, 1968 by Associate Justice Abe Fortas.

The complete text of *Epperson v. Arkansas* can be found in volume 393 of *United States Reports.*

EPPERSON v. ARKANSAS

NOVEMBER 12, 1968

JUSTICE ABE FORTAS delivered the opinion of the Court: This appeal challenges the constitutionality of the "anti-evolution" statute which the State of Arkansas adopted in 1928 to prohibit the teaching in its public schools and universities of the theory that man evolved from other species of life. The statute was a product of the upsurge of "fundamentalist" religious fervor of the twenties. The Arkansas statute was an adaptation of the famous Tennessee "monkey law" which that State adopted in 1925. The constitutionality of the Tennessee law was upheld by the Tennessee Supreme Court in the celebrated *Scopes* case in 1927.

The Arkansas law makes it unlawful for a teacher in any state-supported school or university "to teach the theory or doctrine that mankind ascended or descended from a lower order of animals," or "to adopt or use in any such institution a textbook that teaches" this theory. Violation is a misdemeanor and subjects the violator to dismissal from his position.

The present case concerns the teaching of biology in a high school in Little Rock. According to the testimony, until the events here in litigation, the official textbook furnished for the high school biology course did not have a section on the Darwinian Theory. Then, for the academic year 1965-1966, the school administration, on recommendation of the teachers of biology in the school system, adopted and prescribed a textbook which contained a chapter setting forth "the theory about the origin . . . of man from a lower form of animal."

Susan Epperson, a young woman who graduated from Arkansas' school system and then obtained her master's degree in zoology at the University of Illinois, was employed by the Little Rock system in the fall of 1964 to teach 10th grade biology at Central High School. At the start of the next academic year, 1965, she was confronted by the new textbook (which one surmises from the record was not unwelcome to her). She faced at least a literal dilemma because she was supposed to use the new textbook for classroom instruction and presumably to teach the statutorily condemned chapter; but to do so would be a criminal offense and subject her to dismissal.

She [went before] the Chancery Court of the State, seeking a declaration that the Arkansas statute is void and enjoining [stopping] the State and the defendant officials of the Little Rock school system from dismissing her for violation of the statute's provisions. H.H. Blanchard, a parent of children attending the public schools, intervened in [her] support. . . .

The Chancery Court, in an opinion by Chancellor Murray O. Reid, held that the statute violated the Fourteenth Amendment to the United States Constitution. The court noted that this Amendment encompasses the prohibitions upon state interference with freedom of speech and thought which are contained in the First Amendment. Accordingly, it held that the challenged statute is unconstitutional because, in violation of the First Amendment, it "tends to hinder the quest for knowledge, restrict the freedom to learn, and restrain the freedom to teach." In this perspective, the Act, it held, was an

unconstitutional and void restraint upon the freedom of
speech guaranteed by the Constitution.

On appeal, the Supreme Court of Arkansas reversed [this
decision. In a] two-sentence opinion . . . [i]t sustained
[upheld] the statute as an exercise of the State's power to
specify the curriculum in public schools. It did not
address itself to the . . . constitutional [questions].

Appeal was [made] to this Court. . . . Only Arkansas and
Mississippi have . . . "anti-evolution" or "monkey" laws on
their books. There is no record of any prosecutions in
Arkansas under its statute. It is possible that the statute is
presently more of a curiosity than a vital fact of life in
these States. Nevertheless . . . it is our duty to decide the
issues presented.

At the outset, it is urged upon us that the challenged
statute is vague and uncertain and therefore within the
condemnation of the Due Process Clause of the
Fourteenth Amendment. The contention that the Act is
vague and uncertain is supported by language in the brief
opinion of Arkansas' Supreme Court. That court, perhaps
reflecting the discomfort which the statute's quixotic
prohibition necessarily engenders in the modern mind,
stated that it "expresses no opinion" as to whether the Act
prohibits "explanation" of the theory of evolution or
merely forbids "teaching that the theory is true."
Regardless of this uncertainty, the court held that the
statute is constitutional.

On the other hand, counsel for the State, in oral argument
in this Court, candidly stated that, despite the State
Supreme Court's equivocation, Arkansas would interpret
the statute "to mean that to make a student aware of the

theory . . . just to teach that there was such a theory"
would be grounds for dismissal and for prosecution under
the statute; and he said "that the Supreme Court of
Arkansas' opinion should be interpreted in that manner."
He said: "If Mrs. Epperson would tell her students that
'Here is Darwin's theory, that man ascended or descended
from a lower form of being,' then I think she would be
under this statute liable for prosecution."

In any event, we do not rest our decision upon the
asserted vagueness of the statute. On either interpretation
of its language, Arkansas' statute cannot stand. It is of no
moment whether the law is deemed to prohibit mention of
Darwin's theory, or to forbid any or all of the infinite
varieties of communication embraced within the term
"teaching." Under either interpretation, the law must be
stricken because of its conflict with the constitutional
prohibition of state laws respecting an establishment of
religion or prohibiting the free exercise thereof. The
overriding fact is that Arkansas' law selects from the
body of knowledge a particular segment which it
proscribes for the sole reason that it is deemed to conflict
with a particular religious doctrine; that is, with a
particular interpretation of the Book of Genesis by a
particular religious group.

The antecedents of today's decision are many and
unmistakable. They are rooted in the foundation soil of
our Nation. They are fundamental to freedom.

Government in our democracy, state and national, must be
neutral in matters of religious theory, doctrine, and
practice. It may not be hostile to any religion or to the
advocacy of no-religion; and it may not aid, foster, or
promote one religion or religious theory against another

or even against the militant opposite. The First Amendment mandates governmental neutrality between religion and religion, and between religion and nonreligion.

As early as 1872, this Court said: "The law knows no heresy, and is committed to the support of no dogma, the establishment of no sect." This has been the interpretation of the great First Amendment which this Court has applied in the many and subtle problems which the ferment of our national life has presented for decision within the Amendment's broad command.

Judicial [intrusion] in the operation of the public school system of the Nation raises problems requiring care and restraint. Our courts, however, have not failed to apply the First Amendment's mandate [rule] in our educational system where [it is] essential to safeguard the fundamental values of freedom of speech and inquiry and of belief. By and large, public education in our Nation is committed to the control of state and local authorities. Courts do not and cannot intervene in the resolution of conflicts which arise in the daily operation of school systems and which do not directly and sharply implicate basic constitutional values. On the other hand, "[t]he vigilant protection of constitutional freedoms is nowhere more vital than in the community of American schools." As this Court said in *Keyishian v. Board of Regents*, the First Amendment "does not tolerate laws that cast a pall of orthodoxy over the classroom."

The earliest cases in this Court on the subject of the impact of constitutional guarantees upon the classroom were decided before the Court expressly applied the specific prohibitions of the First Amendment to the

States. But as early as 1923, the Court did not hesitate to condemn under the Due Process Clause "arbitrary" restrictions upon the freedom of teachers to teach and of students to learn. In that year, the Court, in an opinion by Justice McReynolds [in *Meyer v. Nebraska*], held unconstitutional an Act of the State of Nebraska making it a crime to teach any subject in any language other than English to pupils who had not passed the eighth grade. The State's purpose in enacting the law was to promote civic cohesiveness by encouraging the learning of English and to combat the "baneful effect" of permitting foreigners to rear and educate their children in the language of the parents' native land. The Court recognized these purposes, and it acknowledged the State's power to prescribe the school curriculum, but it held that these were not adequate to support the restriction upon the liberty of teacher and pupil. The challenged statute, it held, unconstitutionally interfered with the right of the individual, guaranteed by the Due Process Clause, to engage in any of the common occupations of life and to acquire useful knowledge.

For purposes of the present case, we need not re-enter the difficult terrain which the Court, in 1923, traversed without apparent misgivings. We need not take advantage of the broad premise which the Court's decision in *Meyer* furnishes, nor need we explore the implications of that decision in terms of the justiciability of the multitude of controversies that beset our campuses today. Today's problem is capable of resolution in the narrower terms of the First Amendment's prohibition of laws respecting an establishment of religion or prohibiting the free exercise thereof.

There is and can be no doubt that the First Amendment does not permit the State to require that teaching and learning must be tailored to the principles or prohibitions of any religious sect or dogma. In *Everson v. Board of Education*, this Court, in upholding a state law to provide free bus service to school children, including those attending parochial schools, said: "Neither [a State nor the Federal Government] can pass laws which aid one religion, aid all religions, or prefer one religion, or prefer one religion over another."

At the following Term of Court, in *McCollum v. Board of Education*, the Court held that Illinois could not release pupils from class to attend classes of instruction in the school buildings in the religion of their choice. This, it said, would involve the State in using tax-supported property for religious purposes, thereby breaching the "wall of separation" which, according to Jefferson, the First Amendment was intended to erect between church and state. While study of religions and of the Bible from a literary and historic viewpoint, presented objectively as part of a secular program of education, need not collide with the First Amendment's prohibition, the State may not adopt programs or practices in its public schools or colleges which "aid or oppose" any religion. This prohibition is absolute. It forbids alike the preference of a religious doctrine or the prohibition of theory which is deemed antagonistic to a particular dogma. As Justice Clark stated in *Joseph Burstyn, Inc. v. Wilson*, "the state has no legitimate interest in protecting any or all religions from views distasteful to them. . . ." The test was stated as follows in *Abington School District v. Schempp*, "[W]hat are the purpose and the primary effect of the enactment? If either is the advancement or inhibition of religion then the enactment exceeds the scope of legislative power as circumscribed by the Constitution."

These precedents inevitably determine the result in the present case. The State's undoubted right to prescribe the curriculum for its public schools does not carry with it the right to prohibit, on pain of criminal penalty, the teaching of a scientific theory or doctrine where that prohibition is based upon reasons that violate the First Amendment. It is much too late to argue that the State may impose upon the teachers in its schools any conditions that it chooses, however restrictive they may be of constitutional guarantees.

In the present case, there can be no doubt that Arkansas has sought to prevent its teachers from discussing the theory of evolution because it is contrary to the belief of some that the Book of Genesis must be the exclusive source of doctrine as to the origin of man. No suggestion has been made that Arkansas' law may be justified by considerations of state policy other than the religious views of some of its citizens. It is clear that fundamentalist sectarian conviction was and is the law's reason for existence. Its antecedent, Tennessee's "monkey law," candidly stated its purpose: to make it unlawful "to teach any theory that denies the story of the Divine Creation of man as taught in the Bible, and to teach instead that man has descended from a lower order of animals." Perhaps the sensational publicity attendant upon the *Scopes* trial induced Arkansas to adopt less explicit language. It eliminated Tennessee's reference to "the story of the Divine Creation of man" as taught in the Bible, but there is no doubt that the motivation for the law was the same: to suppress the teaching of a theory which, it was thought, "denied" the divine creation of man.

Arkansas' law cannot be defended as an act of religious neutrality. Arkansas did not seek to excise from the curricula of its schools and universities all discussion of the origin of man. The law's effort was confined to an attempt to blot out a particular theory because of its supposed conflict with the Biblical account, literally read. Plainly, the law is contrary to the mandate [decree] of the First, and in violation of the Fourteenth, Amendment to the Constitution.

The judgment of the Supreme Court of Arkansas is

Reversed.

MONKEY TRIALS

SCOPES v. TENNESSEE

(Forty years before Epperson v. Arkansas *another biology teacher, John T. Scopes, challenged a similar "monkey law" in Tennessee. The appeal from the Scopes Monkey Trial never made it before the U.S. Supreme Court. We present* Scopes *here for its historical significance.)*

In March 1925 the Tennessee Legislature passed a "monkey law," making it illegal to "teach any theory that denies the story of the divine creation of man as taught in the Bible . . . and to teach instead that man had descended from a lower order of animals." The Tennessee Anti-Evolution Act, "an act prohibiting the teaching of the evolution theory . . . and to provide penalties for the violations thereof," punished any teacher found guilty with a fine of not less than one hundred and not more than five hundred dollars.

John Thomas Scopes, a biology teacher, was charged with violating the State's Anti-Evolution Act. The "Scopes Monkey Trial" - basis for the stage play and movie *Inherit The Wind* - took place in Dayton, Tennessee in July 1925. Clarence Darrow, legendary trial lawyer, assisted the defense. William Jennings Bryan, three-time Presidential candidate, assisted the prosecution.

Found guilty of teaching evolution in violation of the Tennessee "monkey law," Scopes was fined one hundred dollars. He appealed his conviction to the Supreme Court of Tennessee on the basis that the Anti-Evolution Act violated both the Tennessee and U.S. Constitutions.

The decision of the Supreme Court of Tennessee was announced on January 17, 1927 by Chief Justice Grafton Green.

The complete text of *Scopes v. Tennessee* can be found in volume 154 of *Tennessee Reports.*

SCOPES v. TENNESSEE

JANUARY 17, 1927

CHIEF JUSTICE GRAFTON GREEN delivered the opinion of the Court: [John] Scopes was convicted of a violation of [Tennessee law], for that he did teach in the public schools of Rhea county a certain theory that denied the story of the divine creation of man, as taught in the Bible, and did teach instead thereof that man had descended from a lower order of animals. After a verdict of guilty by the jury, the trial judge imposed a fine of $100, and Scopes brought the case to this court by an appeal. . . .

While [the Tennessee Anti-Evolution Act] was not drafted with as much care as could have been desired, nevertheless there seems to be no great difficulty in determining its meaning. It is entitled:

> "An act prohibiting the teaching of the evolution theory in all the Universities, normals and all other public schools in Tennessee, which are supported in whole or in part by the public school funds of the state, and to provide penalties for the violations thereof."

Evolution, like prohibition, is a broad term. In recent bickering, however, evolution has been understood to mean the theory which holds that man has developed from some pre-existing lower type. This is the popular significance of evolution, just as the popular significance of prohibition is prohibition of the traffic in intoxicating liquors. It was in that sense that evolution was used in this opinion, unless the context otherwise indicates. It is only to the theory of the evolution of man from a lower type that the act before us was intended to apply, and much of the discussion we have heard is beside this case. The words of a statute, if in common use, are to be taken in their natural and ordinary sense.

Thus defining evolution, this act's title clearly indicates the purpose of the statute to be the prohibition of teaching in the schools of the state that man has developed or descended from some lower type or order of animals.

When the draftsman came to express this purpose in the body of the act, he first forbade the teaching of "any theory that denies the story of the divine creation of man, as taught in the Bible" - his conception evidently being that to forbid the denial of the Bible story would ban the teaching of evolution. To make the purpose more explicit, he added that it should be unlawful to teach "that man has descended from a lower order of animals."

. . . . [T]he act . . . reads that it shall be unlawful for any teacher, etc. -

> "to teach any theory that denies the story of the divine creation of man as taught in the Bible, and to teach instead . . . that man has descended from a lower order of animals."

. . . . The undertaking of the statute was to prevent teaching of the evolution theory. It was considered this purpose could be effected by forbidding the teaching of any theory that denied the Bible story, but to make the

purpose clear it was also forbidden to teach that man
descended from a lower order of animals.

. . . . It . . . seems plain that the Legislature in this
enactment only intended to forbid teaching that men
descended from a lower order of animals. The
denunciation of any theory denying the Bible story of
creation is restricted by the caption and by the final
clause of section 1.

So interpreted, the statute does not seem to be uncertain
in its meaning nor incapable of enforcement for such a
reason, notwithstanding the argument to the contrary.
The indictment [charge] herein follows the language of
the statute. The statute being sufficiently definite in its
terms, such an indictment is good. . . .

It is contended that the statute violates section 8 of article
1 of the Tennessee Constitution, and section 1 of the
Fourteenth Amendment of the Constitution of the United
States - the law of the land clause of the state
Constitution, and the due process of law clause of the
federal Constitution, which are practically equivalent in
meaning.

We think there is little merit in this contention. The
plaintiff [Scopes] was a teacher in the public schools of
Rhea county. He was an employee of the state of
Tennessee or of a municipal agency of the state. He was
under contract with the state to work in an institution of
the state. He had no right or privilege to serve the state
except upon such terms as the state prescribed. His
liberty, his privilege, his immunity to teach and proclaim
the theory of evolution, elsewhere than in the service of
the state, was in no wise touched by this law.

The statute before us is not an exercise of the police power of the state undertaking to regulate the conduct and contracts of individuals in their dealings with each other. On the other hand, it is an act of the state as a corporation, a proprietor, an employer. It is a declaration of a master as to the character of work the master's servant shall, or rather shall not, perform. In dealing with its own employees engaged upon its own work, the state is not hampered by the limitations of section 8 of article 1 of the Tennessee Constitution, nor of the Fourteenth Amendment to the Constitution of the United States.

In *People v. Crane*, the validity of a statute of [New York], providing that citizens only should be employed upon public works was sustained [upheld]. In the course of opinion, it was said:

"'The statute is nothing more, in effect, than a resolve by an employer as to the character of his employees. An individual employer would communicate the resolve to his subordinates by written instructions or by word of mouth. The state, an incorporeal master, speaking through the Legislature, communicates the resolve to its agents by enacting a statute. Either the private employer or the state can revoke the resolve at will. Entire liberty of action in these respects is essential unless the state is to be deprived of a right which has heretofore been deemed a constituent element of the relationship of master and servant, namely, the right of the master to say who his servants shall (and therefore shall not) be."

A case [*Heim v. McCall*] involving the same statute reached the Supreme Court of the United States, and the integrity of the statute was [upheld] by that tribunal. The Supreme Court referred to *People v. Crane*, and approvingly quoted a portion of the language of Chief Judge Barrett that we have set out above.

At the same term of the Supreme Court of the United States an Arizona statute, prohibiting individuals and corporations with more than five workers from employing less than 80 per cent thereof of qualified electors or native-born citizens of the United States was held invalid [in the case of *Truax v. Raich*].

These two cases from the Supreme Court make plain the differing tests to be applied to a statute regulating the state's own affairs and a statute regulating the affairs of private individuals and corporations.

A leading case is *Atkins v. Kansas*. The court there considered and upheld a Kansas statute making it a criminal offense for a contractor for a public work to permit or require an employee to perform labor upon that work in excess of eight hours each day. In that case it was laid down:

"For, whatever may have been the motives controlling the enactment of the statute in question, we can imagine no possible ground to dispute the power of the state to declare that no one undertaking work for it or for one of its municipal agencies, should permit or require an employee on such work to labor in excess of eight hours each day, and to inflict punishment upon those who are embraced by such regulations and yet disregard them.

"It cannot be deemed a part of the liberty of any contractor that he be allowed to do public work in any mode he may choose to adopt, without regard to the wishes of the state. On the contrary, it belongs to the state, as the guardian and trustee for its people, and having control of its affairs, to prescribe the conditions upon which it will permit public work to be done on its behalf, or on behalf of its municipalities. No court has authority to review its action in that respect. Regulations on this subject suggest only considerations of public policy. And with such considerations the courts have no concern."

In *Ellis v. United States, Atkins v. Kansas* was followed, and an act of Congress [was upheld] which prohibited, under penalty of fine or imprisonment, except in case of extraordinary emergency, the requiring or permitting laborers or mechanics employed upon any of the public works of the United States or of the District of Columbia to work more than eight hours each day.

These cases make it obvious that the state or government, as an incident to its power to authorize and enforce contracts for public services, "may require that they shall be carried out only in a way consistent with its views of public policy, and may punish a departure from that way."

To the same effect is *Waugh v. Board of Trustees,* in which a Mississippi statute was sanctioned that prohibited the existence of Greek letter fraternities and similar societies in the state's educational institutions, and

deprived members of such societies of the right to receive
or compete for diplomas, class honors, etc.

This court has indicated a like view in *Leeper v. State*, in
which the constitutionality of . . . the Uniform Text Book
Law was [upheld]. In the opinion in that case Judge
Wilkes observed:

> "If the authority to regulate and control schools is
> legislative, then it . . . must have an unrestricted
> right to prescribe methods, and the courts cannot
> interfere with it unless some scheme is devised
> which is contrary to other provisions of the
> Constitution."

. . . . Since the state may prescribe the character and the
hours of labor of the employees on its works, just as
freely may it say what kind of work shall be performed in
its service, what shall be taught in its schools, so far at
least as section 8 of article 1 of the Tennessee
Constitution, and the Fourteenth Amendment to the
Constitution of the United States, are concerned.

But it is urged that [the Tennessee Anti-Evolution Act]
conflicts with . . . the educational clause, and . . . the
religious clause, of the Tennessee Constitution. It is to be
doubted if [Scopes], before us only as the state's
employee, is sufficiently protected by these constitutional
provisions to justify him in raising such questions.
Nevertheless, as the state appears to concede that these
objections are properly here made, the court will consider
them.

The relevant portion of [the educational clause] of the
Constitution is in these words:

"It shall be the duty of the General Assembly in
all future periods of this government, to cherish
literature and science."

The argument is that the theory of the descent of man
from a lower order of animals is now established by the
preponderance of scientific thought and that the
prohibition of the teaching of such theory is a violation of
the legislative duty to cherish science.

While this clause of the Constitution has been mentioned
in several of our cases, these references have been casual,
and no act of the Legislature has ever been held
inoperative by reason of such provision. . . . To cherish
science means to nourish, to encourage, to foster science.

In no case can the court directly compel the Legislature to
perform its duty. In a plain case the court can prevent
the Legislature from transgressing its duty under the
Constitution by declaring ineffective such a legislative
act. The case, however, must be plain, and the legislative
act is always given the benefit of any doubt.

If a bequest were made to a private trustee with the avails
of which he should cherish science, and there was nothing
more, such a bequest would be void for uncertainty. . . .
A bequest in such terms would be so indefinite that our
courts could not direct a proper application of the trust
fund nor prevent its misapplication. The object of such a
trust could not be ascertained.

If the courts of Tennessee are without power to direct the
administration of such a trust by an individual, how can
they supervise the administration of such a trust by the

Legislature? It is a matter of far more delicacy to undertake the restriction of a coordinate branch of government to the terms of a trust imposed by the Constitution than to confine an individual trustee to the terms of the instrument under which he functions. If language be so indefinite as to preclude judicial restraint of an individual, such language could not possibly excuse judicial restraint of the General Assembly.

If the Legislature thinks that, by reason of popular prejudice, the cause of education and the study of science generally will be promoted by forbidding the teaching of evolution in the schools of the state, we can conceive of no ground to justify the court's interference. The courts cannot sit in judgment on such acts of the Legislature or its agents and determine whether or not the omission or addition of a particular course of study tends "to cherish science."

The last serious criticism made of the act is that it contravenes the provision of . . . the Constitution, "that no preference shall ever be given, by law, to any religious establishment or mode of worship."

The language quoted is a part of our Bill of Rights, was contained in the first Constitution of the state adopted in 1796, and has been brought down into the present Constitution.

At the time of the adoption of our first Constitution, this government had recently been established and the recollection of previous conditions was fresh. England and Scotland maintained state churches as did some of the Colonies, and it was intended by this clause of the

Constitution to prevent any such undertaking in Tennessee.

We are not able to see how the prohibition of teaching the theory that man has descended from a lower order of animals gives preference to any religious establishment or mode of worship. So far as we know, there is no religious establishment or organized body that has in its creed or confession of faith any article denying or affirming such a theory. So far as we know, the denial or affirmation of such a theory does not enter into any recognized mode of worship. Since this [case came before] this court, we have been favored . . . with a multitude of resolutions, addresses, and communications from scientific bodies, religious factions, and individuals giving us the benefit of their views upon the theory of evolution. Examination of these contributions indicates that Protestants, Catholics, and Jews are divided among themselves in their beliefs, and that there is no unanimity among the members of any religious establishment as to this subject. Belief or unbelief in the theory of evolution is no more a characteristic of any religious establishment or mode of worship than is belief or unbelief in the wisdom of the prohibition laws. It would appear that members of the same churches quite generally disagree as to these things.

Furthermore, [the Tennessee Anti-Evolution Act] *requires* the teaching of nothing. It only *forbids* the teaching of the evolution of man from a lower order of animals. [Another Tennessee law] requires that ten verses from the Bible be read each day at the opening of every public school, without comment, and provided the teacher does not read the same verses more than twice during any session. It is also provided in this act that pupils may be

excused from the Bible readings upon the written request
of their parents.

As the law thus stands, while the theory of evolution of
man may not be taught in the schools of the state, nothing
contrary to that theory is required to be taught. It could
scarcely be said that the statutory scriptural reading just
mentioned would amount to teaching of a contrary theory.

Our school authorities are therefore quite free to
determine how they shall act in this state of the law.
Those in charge of the educational affairs of the state are
men and women of discernment and culture. If they
believe that the teaching of the science of biology has
been so hampered by [the Tennessee Anti-Evolution Act]
as to render such an effort no longer desirable, this course
of study may be entirely omitted from the curriculum of
our schools. If this be regarded as a misfortune, it must
be charged to the Legislature. It should be repeated that
the [Tennessee Anti-Evolution Act] deals with nothing
but the evolution of man from a lower order of animals.

It is not necessary now to determine the exact scope of
the religious preference clause of the Constitution and
other language of that section. The situation does not call
for such an attempt. [The religious clause] is binding
alike on the Legislature and the school authorities. So far
we are clear that the Legislature has not crossed these
constitutional limitations. If hereafter the school
authorities should go beyond such limits, a case can then
be brought to the courts.

Much has been said in argument about the motives of the
Legislature in passing this act. But the validity of a

statute must be determined by its natural and legal effect, rather than proclaimed motives.

. . . . This record discloses that the jury found [Scopes] guilty, but did not assess [set] the fine. The trial judge himself undertook to impose the minimum fine of $100 authorized by the statute. This was error. Under . . . the Constitution of Tennessee, a fine in excess of $50 must be assessed by a jury. The statute before us does not permit the imposition of a smaller fine than $100.

Since a jury alone can impose the penalty this act requires, and as a matter of course no different penalty can be inflicted, the trial judge exceeded his jurisdiction in levying this fine, and we are without power to correct his error. The judgment must accordingly be reversed.

The court is informed that [Scopes] is no longer in the service of the state. We see nothing to be gained by prolonging the life of this bizarre case. On the contrary, we think the peace and dignity of the state, which all criminal prosecutions are brought to redress, will be the better conserved by the entry of a nolle prosqui [a statement that no further prosecution will be undertaken] herein. Such a course is suggested to the Attorney General.

SEXUAL HARASSMENT

MERITOR SAVINGS BANK v. VINSON

In 1979 Mechelle Vinson, a female, terminated from her job, filed a sexual harassment suit in Federal Court (based upon Title VII of the Civil Rights Act of 1964) against her former employer, the Meritor Savings Bank, and Sidney Taylor, her former male supervisor.

Vinson charged Taylor with constant verbal and physical public humiliations and with forcing her into a four-year-long involuntary sexual relationship, never reported to the bank because of fear of economic reprisal. Meritor Bank was charged with permitting the existence of a hostile working environment in which such sexual harassment could occur.

At an eleven-day trial in a U.S. District Court, Taylor denied he ever fondled, made suggestive remarks to, or had sexual relations with, Vinson. The bank asserted any sexual harassment of Vinson was unknown to them and was committed without their consent or approval. Taylor and the Bank asserted that Vinson had been terminated in a business-related dispute. The District Court found that if Vinson and Taylor had had an intimate sexual relationship it was voluntary and had nothing to do with her continued employment, and that the Bank could not be held responsible for actions that were unreported.

Vinson appealed the judgment of the District Court to the U.S. Court of Appeals, which reversed the decision based on the U.S. Equal Employment Opportunity Commission's Guideline on Discrimination Because of Sex. Meritor/Taylor appealed this reversal to the U.S. Supreme Court. Oral arguments were heard March 25, 1986 and the decision was announced June 19, 1986 by Associate Justice William Rehnquist.

The complete text of *Meritor Savings Bank v. Vinson* can be found in volume 477 of *United States Reports.*

MERITOR SAVINGS BANK v. VINSON

JUNE 19, 1986

JUSTICE WILLIAM REHNQUIST delivered the opinion of the Court: This case presents important questions concerning claims of workplace "sexual harassment" brought under Title VII of the Civil Rights Act of 1964. . . .

In 1974 . . . Mechelle Vinson met Sidney Taylor, a vice president of . . . Meritor Savings Bank . . . and manager of one of its branch offices. When [Vinson] asked whether she might obtain employment at the bank, Taylor gave her an application, which she completed and returned the next day; later that same day Taylor called her to say that she had been hired. With Taylor as her supervisor, [Vinson] started as a teller-trainee, and thereafter was promoted to teller, head teller, and assistant branch manager. She worked at the same branch for four years, and it is undisputed that her advancement there was based on merit alone. In September 1978, [Vinson] notified Taylor that she was taking sick leave for an indefinite period. On November 1, 1978, the bank discharged her for excessive use of that leave.

[Vinson] brought this action against Taylor and the bank, claiming that during her four years at the bank she had "constantly been subjected to sexual harassment" by Taylor in violation of Title VII. She sought . . . compensatory [compensation for loss caused by an injury] and punitive [above and beyond compensation] damages against Taylor and the bank, and attorney's fees.

At the 11-day . . . trial [in a U.S. District Court], the
parties presented conflicting testimony about Taylor's
behavior during [Vinson]'s employment. [Vinson]
testified that during her probationary period as a teller-
trainee, Taylor treated her in a fatherly way and made no
sexual advances. Shortly thereafter, however, he invited
her out to dinner and, during the course of the meal,
suggested that they go to a motel to have sexual relations.
At first she refused, but out of what she described as fear
of losing her job she eventually agreed. According to
[Vinson], Taylor thereafter made repeated demands upon
her for sexual favors, usually at the branch, both during
and after business hours; she estimated that over the next
several years she had intercourse with him some 40 or 50
times. In addition, [Vinson] testified that Taylor fondled
her in front of other employees, followed her into the
women's restroom when she went there alone, exposed
himself to her, and even forcibly raped her on several
occasions. These activities ceased after 1977, [Vinson]
stated, when she started going with a steady boyfriend.

[Vinson] also testified that Taylor touched and fondled
other women employees of the bank, and she attempted to
call witnesses to support this charge. But while some
supporting testimony apparently was admitted without
objection, the District Court did not allow her "to present
wholesale evidence of a pattern and practice relating to
sexual advances to other female employees in her case in
chief, but advised her that she might well be able to
present such evidence in rebuttal to the defendants'
[Taylor and the bank's] cases." [Vinson] did not offer
such evidence in rebuttal. Finally, [Vinson] testified that
because she was afraid of Taylor she never reported his
harassment to any of his supervisors and never attempted
to use the bank's complaint procedure.

Taylor denied [Vinson]'s allegations of sexual activity, testifying that he never fondled her, never made suggestive remarks to her, never engaged in sexual intercourse with her, and never asked her to do so. He contended instead that [Vinson] made her accusations in response to a business-related dispute. The bank also denied [Vinson]'s allegations and asserted that any sexual harassment by Taylor was unknown to the bank and engaged in without its consent or approval.

The District Court . . . did not resolve the conflicting testimony about the existence of a sexual relationship between [Vinson] and Taylor. It found instead that

> "[i]f [Vinson] and Taylor did engage in an intimate or sexual relationship during the time of [Vinson's] employment with [the bank], that relationship was a voluntary one having nothing to do with her continued employment at [the bank] or her advancement or promotions at that institution."

The Court ultimately found that [Vinson] "was not the victim of sexual harassment and was not the victim of sexual discrimination" while employed at the bank.

Although it concluded that [Vinson] had not proved a violation of Title VII, the District Court nevertheless went on to address the bank's liability. After noting the bank's express policy against discrimination, and finding that neither [Vinson] nor any other employee had ever lodged a complaint about sexual harassment by Taylor, the court ultimately concluded that "the bank was without notice and cannot be held liable for the alleged actions of Taylor."

The Court of Appeals for the District of Columbia Circuit reversed [the District Court's decision]. Relying on its earlier holding in *Bundy v. Jackson*, decided after the trial in this case, the court stated that a violation of Title VII may be predicated on either of two types of sexual harassment: harassment that involves the conditioning of concrete employment benefits on sexual favors, and harassment that, while not affecting economic benefits, creates a hostile or offensive working environment. The court drew additional support for this position from the Equal Employment Opportunity Commission's Guidelines on Discrimination Because of Sex, which set out these two types of sexual harassment claims. Believing that "Vinson's grievance was clearly of the [hostile environment] type," and that the District Court had not considered whether a violation of this type had occurred, the court concluded that a remand [return to the lower court for reconsideration] was necessary.

The court further concluded that the District Court's finding that any sexual relationship between [Vinson] and Taylor "was a voluntary one" did not obviate the need for a remand. "[U]ncertain as to precisely what the [district] court meant" by this finding, the Court of Appeals held that if the evidence otherwise showed that "Taylor made Vinson's toleration of sexual harassment a condition of her employment," her voluntariness "had no materiality whatsoever." The court then surmised that the District Court's finding of voluntariness might have been based on "the voluminous testimony regarding respondent's dress and personal fantasies," testimony that the Court of Appeals believed "had no place in this litigation."

As to the bank's liability, the Court of Appeals held that an employer is absolutely liable for sexual harassment practiced by supervisory personnel, whether or not the employer knew or should have known about the misconduct. The court relied chiefly on Title VII's definition of "employer" to include "any agent of such a person," as well as on the EEOC's Guidelines. The court held that a supervisor is an "agent" of his employer for Title VII purposes, even if he lacks authority to hire, fire, or promote, since "the mere existence - or even the appearance - of a significant degree of influence in vital job decisions gives any supervisor the opportunity to impose on employees."

In accordance with the foregoing, the Court of Appeals reversed the judgment of the District Court and [sent back] the case for further proceedings. A subsequent suggestion for rehearing . . . was denied. . . . We granted certiorari [agreed to hear the case], and now affirm [uphold] but for different reasons.

Title VII of the Civil Rights Act of 1964 makes it "an unlawful employment practice for an employer . . . to discriminate against any individual with respect to his compensation, terms, conditions, or privileges of employment, because of such individual's race, color, religion, sex, or national origin." The prohibition against discrimination based on sex was added to Title VII at the last minute on the floor of the House of Representatives. The principal argument in opposition to the amendment was that "sex discrimination" was sufficiently different from other types of discrimination that it ought to receive separate legislative treatment. This argument was defeated, the bill quickly passed as amended, and we are left with little legislative history to guide us in interpreting the Act's prohibition against discrimination based on "sex."

[Vinson] argues, and the Court of Appeals held, that unwelcome sexual advances that create an offensive or hostile working environment violate Title VII. Without question, when a supervisor sexually harasses a subordinate because of the subordinate's sex, that supervisor "discriminate[s]" on the basis of sex. [The bank] apparently does not challenge this proposition. It contends instead that in prohibiting discrimination with respect to "compensation, terms, conditions, or privileges" of employment, Congress was concerned with what [the bank] describes as "tangible loss" of "an economic character," not "purely psychological aspects of the workplace environment." In support of this claim [the bank] observes that in both the legislative history of Title VII and this Court's Title VII decisions, the focus has been on tangible, economic barriers erected by discrimination.

We reject [the bank]'s view. First, the language of Title VII is not limited to "economic" or "tangible" discrimination. The phrase "terms, conditions, or privileges of employment" evinces a congressional intent "'to strike at the entire spectrum of disparate treatment of men and women'" in employment. [The bank] has pointed to nothing in the Act to suggest that Congress contemplated the limitation urged here.

Second, in 1980 the EEOC issued Guidelines specifying that "sexual harassment," as there defined, is a form of sex discrimination prohibited by Title VII. As an "administrative interpretation of the Act by the enforcing agency," these Guidelines, "'while not controlling upon the courts by reason of their authority, do constitute a body of experience and informed judgment to which courts and litigants may properly resort for guidance.'" The EEOC

Guidelines fully support the view that harassment leading
to noneconomic injury can violate Title VII.

In defining "sexual harassment," the Guidelines first
describe the kinds of workplace conduct that may be
actionable under Title VII. These include "[u]nwelcome
sexual advances, requests for sexual favors, and other
verbal or physical conduct of a sexual nature." Relevant
to the charges at issue in this case, the Guidelines provide
that such sexual misconduct constitutes prohibited "sexual
harassment," whether or not it is directly linked to the
grant or denial of an economic quid pro quo [something
for something], where "such conduct has the purpose or
effect of unreasonably interfering with an individual's
work performance or creating an intimidating, hostile, or
offensive working environment."

In concluding that so-called "hostile environment"
harassment violates Title VII, the EEOC drew upon a
substantial body of judicial decisions and EEOC precedent
holding that Title VII affords employees the right to work
in an environment free from discriminatory intimidation,
ridicule, and insult. *Rogers v. EEOC* was apparently the
first case to recognize a cause of action based upon a
discriminatory work environment. In *Rogers*, the Court
of Appeals for the Fifth Circuit held that a Hispanic
complainant could establish a Title VII violation by
demonstrating that her employer created an offensive
work environment for employees by giving
discriminatory service to its Hispanic clientele. The court
explained that an employee's protections under Title VII
extend beyond the economic aspects of employment:

"[T]he phrase 'terms, conditions or privileges of
employment' in [Title VII] is an expansive

concept which sweeps within its protective ambit the practice of creating a working environment heavily charged with ethnic or racial discrimination. . . . One can readily envision working environments so heavily polluted with discrimination as to destroy completely the emotional and psychological stability of minority group workers. . . ."

Courts applied this principle to harassment based on race, religion, and national origin. Nothing in Title VII suggests that a hostile environment based on discriminatory sexual harassment should not be likewise prohibited. The Guidelines thus appropriately drew from, and were fully consistent with, the existing case law.

Since the Guidelines were issued, courts have uniformly held, and we agree, that a plaintiff may establish a violation of Title VII by proving that discrimination based on sex has created a hostile or abusive work environment. As the Court of Appeals for the Eleventh Circuit wrote in *Henson v. Dundee,*

"Sexual harassment which creates a hostile or offensive environment for members of one sex is every bit the arbitrary barrier to sexual equality at the workplace that racial harassment is to racial equality. Surely, a requirement that a man or woman run a gauntlet of sexual abuse in return for the privilege of being allowed to work and make a living can be as demeaning and disconcerting as the harshest of racial epithets."

Of course, as the courts in both *Rogers* and *Henson* recognized, not all workplace conduct that may be described as "harassment" affects a "term, condition, or privilege" of employment within the meaning of Title VII. For sexual harassment to be actionable, it must be sufficiently severe or pervasive "to alter the conditions of [the victim's] employment and create an abusive working environment." [Vinson]'s allegations in this case - which include not only pervasive harassment but also criminal conduct of the most serious nature - are plainly sufficient to state a claim for "hostile environment" sexual harassment.

The question remains, however, whether the District Court's ultimate finding that [Vinson] "was not the victim of sexual harassment," effectively disposed of [her] claim. The Court of Appeals recognized, we think correctly, that this ultimate finding was likely based on one or both of two erroneous views of the law. First, the District Court apparently believed that a claim for sexual harassment will not lie [without] an *economic* effect on the complainant's employment. ("It is without question that sexual harassment of female employees in which they are asked or required to submit to sexual demands as a *condition to obtain employment or to maintain employment or to obtain promotions* falls within protection of Title VII.") Since it appears that the District Court made its findings without ever considering the "hostile environment" theory of sexual harassment, the Court of Appeals' decision to remand [send the case back to the lower court] was correct.

Second, the District Court's conclusion that no actionable harassment occurred might have rested on its earlier "finding" that "[i]f [Vinson] and Taylor did engage in an intimate or sexual relationship . . . that relationship was a voluntary one." But the fact that sex-related conduct was

"voluntary," in the sense that [Vinson] was not forced to
participate against her will, is not a defense to a sexual
harassment suit brought under Title VII. The [gist] of
any sexual harassment claim is that the alleged sexual
advances were "unwelcome." While the question whether
particular conduct was indeed unwelcome presents
difficult problems of proof and turns largely on
credibility determinations . . . , the District Court in this
case erroneously focused on the "voluntariness" of
[Vinson]'s participation in the claimed sexual episodes.
The correct inquiry is whether [Vinson] by her conduct
indicated that the alleged sexual advances were
unwelcome, not whether her actual participation in sexual
intercourse was voluntary.

[The bank] contends that . . . the Court of Appeals erred
in one of the terms of its [order to send the case back to
the lower court]. Specifically, the Court of Appeals stated
that testimony about [Vinson]'s "dress and personal
fantasies," which the District Court apparently admitted
into evidence, "had no place in this litigation." The
apparent ground for this conclusion was that [Vinson]'s
voluntariness . . . in submitting to Taylor's advances was
immaterial to her sexual harassment claim. While
"voluntariness" in the sense of consent is not a defense to
such a claim, it does not follow that a complainant's
sexually provocative speech or dress is irrelevant . . . in
determining whether he or she found particular sexual
advances unwelcome. To the contrary, such evidence is
obviously relevant. The EEOC Guidelines emphasize that
the trier of fact must determine the existence of sexual
harassment in light of "the record as a whole" and "the
totality of circumstances, such as the nature of the sexual
advances and the context in which the alleged incidents
occurred." . . . While the District Court must carefully

weigh the applicable considerations in deciding whether to admit evidence of this kind, there is no per se rule against its admissibility.

Although the District Court concluded that [Vinson] had not proved a violation of Title VII, it nevertheless went on to consider the question of the bank's liability. Finding that "the bank was without notice" of Taylor's alleged conduct, and that notice to Taylor was not the equivalent of notice to the bank, the court concluded that the bank therefore could not be held liable for Taylor's alleged actions. The Court of Appeals took the opposite view, holding that an employer is strictly liable for a hostile environment created by a supervisor's sexual advances, even though the employer neither knew nor reasonably could have known of the alleged misconduct. The court held that a supervisor, whether or not he possesses the authority to hire, fire, or promote, is necessarily an "agent" of his employer for all Title VII purposes, since "even the appearance" of such authority may enable him to impose himself on his subordinates.

. . . [S]everal different standards for employer liability [are suggested. Vinson], not surprisingly, defends the position of the Court of Appeals. Noting that Title VII's definition of "employer" includes any "agent" of the employer, she also argues that "so long as the circumstance is work-related, the supervisor is the employer and the employer is the supervisor." Notice to Taylor that the advances were unwelcome, therefore, was notice to the bank.

[The bank] argues that [Vinson]'s failure to use its established grievance procedure, or to otherwise put it on notice of the alleged misconduct, insulates [the bank] from liability for Taylor's wrongdoing. A contrary rule would be unfair, [the bank] argues, since in a hostile environment harassment case the employer often will have no reason to know about, or opportunity to cure, the alleged wrongdoing.

The EEOC ... contends that courts formulating employer liability rules should draw from traditional agency principles. Examination of those principles has led the EEOC to the view that where a supervisor exercises the authority actually delegated to him by his employer, by making or threatening to make decisions affecting the employment status of his subordinates, such actions are properly imputed to the employer whose delegation of authority empowered the supervisor to undertake them. Thus, the courts have consistently held employers liable for the discriminatory discharges of employees by supervisory personnel, whether or not the employer knew, should have known, or approved of the supervisor's actions.

The EEOC suggests that when a sexual harassment claim rests exclusively on a "hostile environment" theory, however, the usual basis for a finding of agency will often disappear. In that case, the EEOC believes, agency principles lead to

"a rule that asks whether a victim of sexual harassment had reasonably available an avenue of complaint regarding such harassment, and, if available and utilized, whether that procedure was reasonably responsive to the employee's complaint. If the employer has an expressed policy against sexual harassment and has implemented a procedure specifically designed to resolve sexual harassment claims, and if the victim does not take advantage of that procedure, the employer should be shielded from liability absent actual knowledge of the sexually hostile environment (obtained, e.g., by the filing of a charge with the EEOC or a comparable state agency). In all other cases, the employer will be liable if it has actual knowledge of the harassment or if, considering all the facts of the case, the victim in question had no reasonably available avenue for making his or her complaint known to appropriate management officials."

As [Vinson] points out, this suggested rule is in some tension with the EEOC Guidelines, which hold an employer liable for the acts of its agents without regard to notice. The Guidelines do require, however, an "examin[ation of] the circumstances of the particular employment relationship and the job [f]unctions performed by the individual in determining whether an individual acts in either a supervisory or agency capacity."

This debate over the appropriate standard for employer liability has a rather abstract quality about it given the state of the record in this case. We do not know at this stage whether Taylor made any sexual advances toward [Vinson] at all, let alone whether those advances were unwelcome, whether they were sufficiently pervasive to constitute a condition of employment, or whether they were "so pervasive and so long continuing . . . that the employer must have become conscious of [them]."

We therefore decline the parties' invitation to issue a definitive rule on employer liability, but we do agree with the EEOC that Congress wanted courts to look to agency principles for guidance in this area. While such common-law principles may not be transferable in all their particulars to Title VII, Congress' decision to define "employer" to include any "agent" of an employer surely evinces an intent to place some limits on the acts of employees for which employers under Title VII are to be held responsible. For this reason, we hold that the Court of Appeals erred in concluding that employers are always automatically liable for sexual harassment by their supervisors. For the same reason, absence of notice to an employer does not necessarily insulate that employer from liability.

Finally, we reject [the bank]'s view that the mere existence of a grievance procedure and a policy against discrimination, coupled with [Vinson]'s failure to invoke that procedure, must insulate [the bank] from liability. . . . [The bank]'s general nondiscrimination policy did not address sexual harassment in particular, and thus did not alert employees to their employer's interest in correcting that form of discrimination. Moreover, the bank's grievance procedure apparently required an employee to complain first to her supervisor, in this case Taylor. Since Taylor was the alleged perpetrator, it is not altogether surprising that [Vinson] failed to invoke the procedure and report her grievance to him. [The bank]'s contention that [Vinson]'s failure should insulate it from liability might be substantially stronger if its procedures were better calculated to encourage victims of harassment to come forward.

In sum, we hold that a claim of "hostile environment" sex discrimination is actionable under Title VII, that the District Court's findings were insufficient to dispose of [Vinson]'s hostile environment claim, and that the District

Court did not err in admitting testimony about [Vinson]'s sexually provocative speech and dress. As to employer liability, we conclude that the Court of Appeals was wrong to entirely disregard agency principles and impose absolute liability on employers for the acts of their supervisors, regardless of the circumstances of a particular case.

Accordingly, the judgment of the Court of Appeals reversing the judgment of the District Court is affirmed [upheld], and the case is [sent back] for further proceedings consistent with this opinion.

It is so ordered.

CHURCH & STATE

ALLEGHENY COUNTY v. ACLU

From late November 1986 through mid-January 1987 a creche, depicting the Christian nativity scene, and a menorah, commemorating the Jewish holiday of Chanukah, were permitted to be placed on public property in downtown Pittsburgh, Pennsylvania.

The creche, including figures of the infant Jesus, Mary, Joseph, and an angel with a banner proclaiming: "Glory To God In The Highest!" was placed inside the Allegheny County Courthouse. The display was sponsored by the Holy Name Society, a Roman Catholic group.

The menorah, an eighteen-foot-high candelabra, was placed outside the entrance to the City-County Building. The display was sponsored by Chabad, a Jewish group.

On December 10, 1986 the Greater Pittsburgh Chapter of the American Civil Liberties Union (ACLU) filed suit against the City of Pittsburgh and Allegheny County to permanently halt the annual displays, permitted since 1981, of the creche and menorah. The ACLU suit was based on the Constitutional separation of church and state.

A U.S. District Court ruled May 8, 1987 in favor of the City and County. The ACLU appealed and won a reversal on March 15, 1988 from the U.S. Court of Appeals. The City and County then appealed to the U.S. Supreme Court, which agreed to a review on December 12, 1988.

Oral arguments were heard before the Court February 22, 1989 and a decision was announced on July 3, 1989 by Associate Justice Harry Blackmun.

The complete text of *Allegheny County v American Civil Liberties Union* can be found in volume 492 of *United States Reports*.

ALLEGHENY COUNTY v. ACLU

JULY 3, 1989

JUSTICE HARRY BLACKMUN delivered the opinion of the Court: This litigation concerns the constitutionality of two recurring holiday displays located on public property in downtown Pittsburgh. The first is a creche placed on the Grand Staircase of the Allegheny County Courthouse. The second is a Chanukah menorah placed just outside the City-County Building, next to a Christmas tree and a sign saluting liberty. The Court of Appeals for the Third circuit ruled that each display violates the Establishment Clause of the First Amendment because each has the impermissible effect of endorsing religion. We agree that the creche display has that unconstitutional effect but reverse the Court of Appeals' judgment regarding the menorah display.

The County Courthouse is owned by Allegheny County and is its seat of government. It houses the offices of the County Commissioners, Controller, Treasurer, Sheriff, and Clerk of Court. Civil and criminal trials are held there. The "main," "most beautiful," and "most public" part of the courthouse is its Grand Staircase, set into one arch and surrounded by others, with arched windows serving as a backdrop.

Since 1981, the county has permitted the Holy Name Society, a Roman Catholic group, to display a creche in the County Courthouse during the Christmas holiday season. Christmas, we note perhaps needlessly, is the holiday when Christians celebrate the birth of Jesus of

Nazareth, whom they believe to be the Messiah. Western churches have celebrated Christmas Day on December 25 since the fourth century. As observed in this Nation, Christmas has a secular as well as a religious dimension.

The creche in the County Courthouse, like other creches, is a visual representation of the scene in the manger in Bethlehem shortly after the birth of Jesus, as described in the Gospels of Luke and Matthew. The creche includes figures of the infant Jesus, Mary, Joseph, farm animals, shepherds, and wise men, all placed in or before a wooden representation of a manger, which has at its crest an angel bearing a banner that proclaims "Gloria in Excelsis Deo!"

During the 1986-1987 holiday season, the creche was on display on the Grand Staircase from November 26 to January 9. It had a wooden fence on three sides and bore a plaque stating: "This Display Donated by the Holy Name Society." Sometime during the week of December 2, the county placed red and white poinsettia plants around the fence. The county also placed a small evergreen tree, decorated with a red bow, behind each of the two endposts of the fence. These trees stood alongside the manger backdrop, and were slightly shorter than it was. The angel thus was at the apex of the creche display. Altogether, the creche, the fence, the poinsettias, and the trees occupied a substantial amount of space on the Grand Staircase. No figures of Santa Claus or other decorations appeared on the Grand Staircase.

The county uses the creche as the setting for its annual Christmas-carol program. During the 1986 season, the county invited high school choirs and other musical groups to perform during weekday lunch hours from December 3 through December 23. The county dedicated this program to world peace and to the families of prisoners-of-war and of persons missing-in-action in Southeast Asia.

Near the Grand Staircase is an area of the County Courthouse known as the "gallery forum" used for art and other cultural exhibits. The creche, with its fence-and-floral frame, however, was distinct and not connected with any exhibit in the gallery forum. In addition, various departments and offices within the County Courthouse had their own Christmas decorations, but these also are not visible from the Grand Staircase. The City-County Building is separate and a block removed from the County Courthouse and, as the name implies, is jointly owned by the city of Pittsburgh and Allegheny County. The city's portion of the building houses the city's principal offices, including the Mayor's. The city is responsible for the building's Grant Street entrance which has three rounded arches supported by columns.

For a number of years, the city has had a large Christmas tree under the middle arch outside the Grant Street entrance. Following this practice, city employees on November 17, 1986, erected a 45-foot tree under the middle arch and decorated it with lights and ornaments. A few days later, the city placed at the foot of the tree a sign bearing the Mayor's name and entitled "Salute to Liberty." Beneath the title, the sign stated:

> "During this holiday season, the City of Pittsburgh salutes liberty. Let these festive lights remind us that we are the keepers of the flame of liberty and our legacy of freedom."

At least since 1982, the city has expanded its Grant Street
holiday display to include a symbolic representation of
Chanukah, an 8-day Jewish holiday that begins on the
25th day of the Jewish lunar month of Kislev. The 15th
of Kislev usually occurs in December, and thus Chanukah
is the annual Jewish holiday that falls closest to Christmas
Day each year. In 1986, Chanukah began at sundown on
December 26.

According to Jewish tradition, on the 25th of Kislev in
164 B.C.E. (before the common era), the Maccabees
rededicated the Temple of Jerusalem after recapturing it
from the Greeks, or, more accurately, from the Greek-
influenced Seleucid Empire, in the course of a political
rebellion. Chanukah is the holiday which celebrates that
event. The early history of the celebration of Chanukah
is unclear; it appears that the holiday's central ritual - the
lighting of lamps - was well established long before a
single explanation of that ritual took hold.

The Talmud [a book of Jewish law] explains that
lamplighting ritual as a commemoration of an event that
occurred during the rededication of the Temple. The
Temple housed a seven-branch menorah, which was to be
kept burning continuously. When the Maccabees
rededicated the Temple, they had only enough oil to last
for one day. But, according to the Talmud, the oil
miraculously lasted for eight days (the length of time it
took to obtain additional oil). To celebrate and publicly
proclaim this miracle, the Talmud prescribes that it is a
mitzvah (i.e., a religious deed or commandment) for Jews
to place a lamp with eight lights just outside the entrance
to their homes during the eight days of Chanukah. Where
practicality or safety from persecution so requires, the

lamp may be placed in a window or inside the home. The Talmud also ordains certain blessings to be recited each night of Chanukah before lighting the lamp. One such benediction has been translated into English as "We are blessing God who has sanctified us and commanded us with mitzvot and has told us to light the candles of Hanukkah."

Although Jewish law does not contain any rule regarding the shape or substance of a Chanukah lamp (or "hanukkiyah"), it became customary to evoke the memory of the Temple menorah. The Temple menorah was of a tree-and-branch design; it had a central candlestick with six branches. In contrast, a Chanukah menorah of tree-and-branch design has eight branches - one for each day of the holiday - plus a ninth to hold the shamash (an extra candle used to light the other eight). Also in contrast to the Temple menorah, the Chanukah menorah is not a sanctified object; it need not be treated with special care.

Lighting the menorah is the primary tradition associated with Chanukah, but the holiday is marked by other traditions as well. One custom among some Jews is to give children Chanukah gelt, or money. Another is for the children to gamble their gelt using a dreidel, a top with four sides. Each of the four sides contains a Hebrew letter; together the four letters abbreviate a phrase that refers to the Chanukah miracle.

Chanukah, like Christmas, is a cultural event as well as a religious holiday. Indeed, the Chanukah story always has had a political or national as well as a religious dimension: it tells of national heroism in addition to divine intervention. Also, Chanukah, like Christmas, is a winter holiday; according to some historians, it was associated in

ancient times with the winter solstice. Just as some
Americans celebrate Christmas without regard to its
religious significance, some nonreligious American Jews
celebrate Chanukah as an expression of ethnic identity,
and "as a cultural or national event, rather than as a
specifically religious event."

The cultural significance of Chanukah varies with the
setting in which the holiday is celebrated. In
contemporary Israel, the nationalist and military aspects
of the Chanukah story receive special emphasis. In this
country, the tradition of giving Chanukah gelt has taken
on greater importance because of the temporal proximity
of Chanukah to Christmas. Indeed, some have suggested
that the proximity of Christmas accounts for the social
prominence of Chanukah in this country. Whatever the
reason, Chanukah is observed by American Jews to an
extent greater than its religious importance would
indicate: in the hierarchy of Jewish holidays, Chanukah
ranks fairly low in religious significance. This socially
heightened status of Chanukah reflects its cultural or
secular dimension.

On December 22 of the 1986 holiday season, the city
placed at the Grant Street entrance to the City-County
Building an 18-foot Chanukah menorah of an abstract
tree-and-branch design. The menorah was placed next to
the city's 45-foot Christmas tree, against one of the
columns that supports the arch into which the tree was
set. The menorah is owned by Chabad, a Jewish group,
but is stored, erected, and removed each year by the city.
The tree, the sign, and the menorah were all removed on
January 13. . . .

This litigation began on December 10, 1986, when respondents the Greater Pittsburgh Chapter of the American Civil Liberties Union [ACLU] and seven local residents, filed suit against the county and the city, seeking permanently to enjoin [stop] the county from displaying the creche in the County Courthouse and the city from displaying the menorah in front of the City-County Building. [The ACLU] claim[s] that the displays of the creche and the menorah each violate the Establishment Clause of the First Amendment, made applicable to state governments by the Fourteenth Amendment. Chabad was permitted to intervene to defend the display of its menorah.

On May 8, 1987, the District Court denied [the ACLU]'s request for a permanent injunction [court order to prohibit an act]. Relying on *Lynch v. Donnelly*, the court stated that "the creche was but part of the holiday decoration of the stairwell and a foreground for the highschool choirs which entertained each day at noon." Regarding the menorah, the court concluded that "it was but an insignificant part of another holiday display." The court also found that "the displays had a secular purpose" and "did not create an excessive entanglement of government with religion."

. . . . [A] divided panel of the Court of Appeals reversed [the decision]. . . . [T]he panel majority determined that the creche and the menorah must be understood as endorsing Christianity and Judaism. The court observed: "Each display was located at or in a public building devoted to core functions of government." The court also stated: "Further, while the menorah was placed near a Christmas tree, neither the creche nor the menorah can reasonably be deemed to have been subsumed by a larger

display of non-religious items." Because the
impermissible effect of endorsing religion was a
sufficient basis for holding each display to be in violation
of the Establishment Clause under *Lemon v. Kurtzman,*
the Court of Appeals did not consider whether either one
had an impermissible purpose or resulted in an
unconstitutional entanglement between government and
religion.

The dissenting judge stated that the creche, "accompanied
by poinsettia plants and evergreens, does not violate the
Establishment Clause simply because plastic Santa Clauses
or reindeer are absent." As to the menorah, he asserted:
"Including a reference to Chanukah did no more than
broaden the commemoration of the holiday season and
stress the notion of sharing its joy."

. . . . The county, the city, and Chabad each filed a
petition for certiorari [asked the Supreme Court to review
the cases]. We granted all three petitions.

This Nation is heir to a history and tradition of religious
diversity that dates from the settlement of the North
American continent. Sectarian differences among various
Christian denominations were central to the origins of our
Republic. Since then, adherents of religions too numerous
to name have made the United States their home, as have
those whose beliefs expressly exclude religion.

Precisely because of the religious diversity that is our
national heritage, the Founders added to the Constitution
a Bill of Rights, the very first words of which declare:
"Congress shall make no law respecting an establishment
of religion, or prohibiting the free exercise thereof . . ."
Perhaps in the early days of the Republic these words

were understood to protect only the diversity within Christianity, but today they are recognized as guaranteeing religious liberty and equality to "the infidel, the atheist, or the adherent of a non-Christian faith such as Islam or Judaism." It is settled law that no government official in this Nation may violate these fundamental constitutional rights regarding matters of conscience.

. . . . [T]his Court has come to understand the Establishment Clause to mean that government may not promote or affiliate itself with any religious doctrine or organization, may not discriminate among persons on the basis of their religious beliefs and practices, may not delegate a governmental power to a religious institution, and may not involve itself too deeply in such an institution's affairs. . . . [I]n *Everson v. Board of Education*, the Court gave this often-repeated summary:

> "The 'establishment of religion' clause of the First Amendment means at least this: Neither a state nor the Federal Government can set up a church. Neither can pass laws which aid one religion, aid all religions, or prefer one religion over another. Neither can force nor influence a person to go to or remain away from church against his will or force him to profess a belief or disbelief in any religion. No person can be punished for entertaining or professing religious beliefs or disbeliefs, for church attendance or non-attendance. No tax in any amount, large or small, can be levied to support any religious activities or institutions, whatever they may be called, or whatever form they may adopt to teach or practice religion. Neither a state nor the Federal Government can, openly or secretly,

participate in the affairs of any religious
organizations or groups and vice versa."

In *Lemon v. Kurtzman*, the Court sought to refine these
principles by focusing on three "tests" for determining
whether a government practice violates the Establishment
Clause. Under the *Lemon* analysis, a statute or practice
which touches upon religion, if it is to be permissible
under the Establishment Clause, must have a secular
purpose; it must neither advance nor inhibit religion in its
principal or primary effect; and it must not foster an
excessive entanglement with religion. This trilogy of tests
has been applied regularly in the Court's later
Establishment Clause cases.

Our subsequent decisions further have refined the
definition of governmental action that unconstitutionally
advances religion. In recent years, we have paid
particularly close attention to whether the challenged
governmental practice either has the purpose or effect of
"endorsing" religion, a concern that has long had a place
in our Establishment Clause jurisprudence. Thus, in
Wallace v. Jaffree, the Court held unconstitutional
Alabama's moment-of-silence statute because it was
"enacted . . . for the sole purpose of expressing the State's
endorsement of prayer activities." The Court similarly
invalidated Louisiana's "Creationism Act" because it
"endorses religion" in its purpose. And the educational
program in *School District of Grand Rapids v. Ball* was
held to violate the Establishment Clause because of its
"endorsement" effect.

Of course, the word "endorsement" is not self-defining.
Rather, it derives its meaning from other words that this
Court has found useful over the years in interpreting the

Establishment Clause. Thus, it has been noted that the prohibition against governmental endorsement of religion "preclude[s] government from conveying or attempting to convey a message that religion or a particular religious belief is *favored or preferred.*" Moreover, the term "endorsement" is closely linked to the term "promotion," and this Court long since has held that government "may not . . . promote one religion or religious theory against another or even against the militant opposite."

Whether the key word is "endorsement," "favoritism," or "promotion," the essential principle remains the same. The Establishment Clause, at the very least, prohibits government from appearing to take a position on questions of religious belief or from "making adherence to a religion relevant in any way to a person's standing in the political community."

We have had occasion in the past to apply Establishment Clause principles to the government's display of objects with religious significance. In *Stone v. Graham,* we held that the display of a copy of the Ten Commandments on the walls of public classrooms violates the Establishment Clause. Closer to the facts of this litigation is *Lynch v. Donnelly,* in which we considered whether the city of Pawtucket, R.I., had violated the Establishment Clause by including a creche in its annual Christmas display, located in a private park within the downtown shopping district. By a 5-4 decision in that difficult case, the Court upheld inclusion of the creche in the Pawtucket display, holding . . . that the inclusion of the creche did not have the impermissible effect of advancing or promoting religion.

The rationale of the majority opinion in *Lynch* is none too clear. . . . First, the opinion states that the inclusion of

the creche in the display was "no more an advancement or
endorsement of religion" than other "endorsements" this
Court has approved in the past, but the opinion offers no
discernible   measure   for   distinguishing   between
permissible and impermissible endorsements. Second, the
opinion observes that any benefit the government's
display of the creche gave to religion was no more than
"indirect, remote, and incidental," without saying how or
why.

Although Justice O'Connor joined the majority opinion in
Lynch, she wrote a concurrence that differs in significant
respects from the majority opinion. The main difference
is that the concurrence provides a sound analytical
framework for evaluating governmental use of religious
symbols.

First and foremost, the concurrence squarely rejects any
notion that this Court will tolerate some government
endorsement of religion.   Rather, the concurrence
recognizes any endorsement of religion as "invalid"
because it "sends a message to nonadherents that they are
outsiders, not full members of the political community,
and an accompanying message to adherents that they are
insiders, favored members of the political community."

Second, the concurrence articulates a method for
determining whether the government's use of an object
with religious meaning has the effect of endorsing
religion.   The effect of the display depends upon the
message that the government's practice communicates: the
question is "what viewers may fairly understand to be the
purpose of the display." That inquiry, of necessity, turns
upon the context in which the contested object appears: "a
typical museum setting, though not neutralizing the

religious content of a religious painting, negates any message of endorsement of that content." The concurrence thus emphasizes that the constitutionality of the creche in that case depended upon its "particular physical setting," and further observes: "Every government practice must be judged in its unique circumstances to determine whether it [endorses] religion."

The concurrence applied this mode of analysis to the Pawtucket creche, seen in the context of that city's holiday celebration as a whole. In addition to the creche, the city's display contained: a Santa Claus House with a live Santa distributing candy; reindeer pulling Santa's sleigh; a live 40-foot Christmas tree strung with lights; statues of carolers in old-fashioned dress; candy-striped poles; a "talking" wishing well; a large banner proclaiming "SEASONS GREETINGS"; a miniature "village" with several houses and a church; and various "cut-out" figures, including those of a clown, a dancing elephant, a robot, and a teddy bear. The concurrence concluded that both because the creche is "a traditional symbol" of Christmas, a holiday with strong secular elements, and because the creche was "displayed along with purely secular symbols," the creche's setting "changes what viewers may fairly understand to be the purpose of the display" and "negates any message of endorsement" of "the Christian beliefs represented by the creche."

The four *Lynch* dissenters agreed with the concurrence that the controlling question was "whether Pawtucket ha[d] run afoul of the Establishment Clause by endorsing religion through its display of the creche." The dissenters also agreed with the general proposition that the context in which the government uses a religious symbol is relevant for determining the answer to that question. They simply reached a different answer: the dissenters concluded that the other elements of the Pawtucket display did not negate the endorsement of Christian faith caused by the presence of the creche. They viewed the inclusion of the creche in the city's overall display as placing "the government's imprimatur of approval on the particular religious beliefs exemplified by the creche." Thus, they stated: "The effect on minority religious groups, as well as on those who may reject all religion, is to convey the message that their views are not similarly worthy of public recognition nor entitled to public support."

Thus, despite divergence at the bottom line, the five Justices in concurrence and dissent in *Lynch* agreed upon the relevant constitutional principles: the government's use of religious symbolism is unconstitutional if it has the effect of endorsing religious beliefs, and the effect of the government's use of religious symbolism depends upon its context. These general principles are sound, and have been adopted by the Court in subsequent cases. Since *Lynch*, the Court has made clear that, when evaluating the effect of government conduct under the Establishment Clause, we must ascertain whether "the challenged governmental action is sufficiently likely to be perceived by adherents of the controlling denominations as an endorsement, and by the nonadherents as a disapproval, of their individual religious choices." Accordingly, our present task is to determine whether the display of the creche and the menorah, in their respective "particular physical settings," has the effect of endorsing or disapproving religious beliefs.

We turn first to the county's creche display. There is no doubt, of course, that the creche itself is capable of communicating a religious message. Indeed, the creche in this lawsuit uses words, as well as the picture of the nativity scene, to make its religious meaning unmistakably clear. "Glory to God in the Highest!" says the angel in the creche - Glory to God because of the birth of Jesus. This praise to God in Christian terms is indisputably religious - indeed sectarian - just as it is when said in the Gospel or in a church service.

Under the Court's holding in *Lynch*, the effect of a creche display turns on its setting. Here, unlike in *Lynch*, nothing in the context of the display detracts from the creche's religious message. The *Lynch* display comprised a series of figures and objects, each group of which had its own focal point. . . . Here, in contrast, the creche stands alone: it is the single element of the display on the Grand Staircase.

The floral decoration surrounding the creche cannot be viewed as somehow equivalent to the secular symbols in the overall *Lynch* display. The floral frame, like all good frames, serves only to draw one's attention to the message inside the frame. The floral decoration surrounding the creche contributes to, rather than detracts from, the endorsement of religion conveyed by the creche. It is as if the county had allowed the Holy Name Society to display a cross on the Grand Staircase at Easter, and the county had surrounded the cross with Easter lilies. The county could not say that surrounding the cross with traditional flowers of the season would negate the endorsement of Christianity conveyed by the cross on the Grand Staircase. Its contention that the traditional

Christmas greens negate the endorsement effect of the creche fares no better.

Nor does the fact that the creche was the setting for the county's annual Christmas-carol program diminish its religious meaning. First, the carol program in 1986 lasted only from December 3 to December 23 and occupied at most two hours a day. The effect of the creche on those who viewed it when the choirs were not singing - the vast majority of the time - cannot be negated by the presence of the choir program. Second, because some of the carols performed at the site of the creche were religious in nature, those carols were more likely to augment the religious quality of the scene than to secularize it.

Furthermore, the creche sits on the Grand Staircase, the "main" and "most beautiful part" of the building that is the seat of county government.   No viewer could reasonably think that it occupies this location without the support and approval of the government.   Thus, by permitting the "display of the creche in this particular physical setting,"   the county sends an unmistakable message that it supports and promotes the Christian praise to God that is the creche's religious message.

The fact that the creche bears a sign disclosing its ownership by a Roman Catholic organization does not alter this conclusion. On the contrary, the sign simply demonstrates that the government is endorsing the religious message of that organization, rather than communicating a message of its own.   But the Establishment Clause does not limit only the religious content of the government's own communications. It also prohibits the government's support and promotion of religious communications by religious organizations.

Indeed, the very concept of "endorsement" conveys the sense of promoting someone else's message. Thus, by prohibiting government endorsement of religion, the Establishment Clause prohibits precisely what occurred here: the government's lending its support to the communication of a religious organization's religious message.

Finally, the county argues that it is sufficient to validate the display of the creche on the Grand Staircase that the display celebrates Christmas, and Christmas is a national holiday. This argument obviously proves too much. It would allow the celebration of the Eucharist inside a courthouse on Christmas Eve. While the county may have doubts about the constitutional status of celebrating the Eucharist inside the courthouse under the government's auspices, this Court does not. The government may acknowledge Christmas as a cultural phenomenon, but under the First Amendment it may not observe it as a Christian holy day by suggesting that people praise God for the birth of Jesus.

In sum, *Lynch* teaches that government may celebrate Christmas in some manner and form, but not in a way that endorses Christian doctrine. Here, Allegheny County has transgressed this line. It has chosen to celebrate Christmas in a way that has the effect of endorsing a patently Christian message: Glory to God for the birth of Jesus Christ. Under *Lynch,* and the rest of our cases, nothing more is required to demonstrate a violation of the Establishment Clause. The display of the creche in this context, therefore, must be permanently enjoined [stopped].

. . . . To be sure, in a pluralistic society there may be some would-be theocrats, who wish that their religion were an established creed, and some of them perhaps may be even audacious enough to claim that the lack of established religion discriminates against their preferences. But this claim gets no relief, for it contradicts the fundamental premise of the Establishment Clause itself. The antidiscrimination principle inherent in the Establishment Clause necessarily means that would-be discriminators on the basis of religion cannot prevail.

For this reason, the claim that prohibiting government from celebrating Christmas as a religious holiday discriminates against Christians in favor of nonadherents must fail. Celebrating Christmas as a religious, as opposed to a secular, holiday, necessarily entails professing, proclaiming, or believing that Jesus of Nazareth, born in a manger in Bethlehem, is the Christ, the Messiah. If the government celebrates Christmas as a religious holiday (for example, by issuing an official proclamation saying: "We rejoice in the glory of Christ's birth!"), it means that the government really is declaring Jesus to be the Messiah, a specifically Christian belief. In contrast, confining the government's own celebration of Christmas to the holiday's secular aspects does *not* favor the religious beliefs of non-Christians over those of Christians. Rather, it simply permits the government to acknowledge the holiday without expressing an allegiance to Christian beliefs, an allegiance that would truly favor Christians over non-Christians. To be sure, some Christians may wish to see the government proclaim its allegiance to Christianity in a religious celebration of Christmas, but the Constitution does not permit the gratification of that desire, which would contradict "'the logic of secular liberty'" it is the purpose of the Establishment Clause to protect.

Of course, not all religious celebrations of Christmas located on government property violate the Establishment Clause. It obviously is not unconstitutional, for example, for a group of parishioners from a local church to go caroling through a city park on any Sunday in Advent or for a Christian club at a public university to sing carols during their Christmas meeting. The reason is that activities of this nature do not demonstrate the government's allegiance to, or endorsement of, the Christian faith.

Equally obvious, however, is the proposition that not all proclamations of Christian faith located on government property are permitted by the Establishment Clause just because they occur during the Christmas holiday season, as the example of a Mass in the courthouse surely illustrates. And once the judgment has been made that a particular proclamation of Christian belief, when disseminated from a particular location on government property, has the effect of demonstrating the government's endorsement of Christian faith, then it necessarily follows that the practice must be [stopped] to protect the constitutional rights of those citizens who follow some creed other than Christianity. It is thus incontrovertible that the Court's decision today, premised on the determination that the creche display on the Grand Staircase demonstrates the county's endorsement of Christianity, does not represent a hostility or indifference to religion but, instead, the respect for religious diversity that the Constitution requires.

The display of the Chanukah menorah in front of the City-County Building may well present a closer constitutional question. The menorah, one must recognize, is a religious symbol: it serves to commemorate the miracle of the oil as described in the Talmud. But the menorah's message is not exclusively religious. The menorah is the primary visual symbol for a holiday that, like Christmas, has both religious and secular dimensions.

Moreover, the menorah here stands next to a Christmas tree and a sign saluting liberty. While no challenge has been made here to the display of the tree and the sign, their presence is obviously relevant in determining the effect of the menorah's display. The necessary result of placing a menorah next to a Christmas tree is to create an "overall holiday setting" that represents both Christmas and Chanukah - two holidays, not one.

The mere fact that Pittsburgh displays symbols of both Christmas and Chanukah does not end the constitutional inquiry. If the city celebrates both Christmas and Chanukah as religious holidays, then it violates the Establishment Clause. The simultaneous endorsement of Judaism and Christianity is no less constitutionally infirm than the endorsement of Christianity alone.

Conversely, if the city celebrates both Christmas and Chanukah as secular holidays, then its conduct is beyond the reach of the Establishment Clause. Because government may celebrate Christmas as a secular holiday, it follows that government may also acknowledge Chanukah as a secular holiday. Simply put, it would be a form of discrimination against Jews to allow Pittsburgh to celebrate Christmas as a cultural tradition while simultaneously disallowing the city's acknowledgment of Chanukah as a contemporaneous cultural tradition.

Accordingly, the relevant question for Establishment Clause purposes is whether the combined display of the tree, the sign, and the menorah has the effect of endorsing both Christian and Jewish faiths, or rather simply recognizes that both Christmas and Chanukah are part of the same winter-holiday season, which has attained a secular status in our society. Of the two interpretations of this particular display, the latter seems far more plausible. . . .

The Christmas tree, unlike the menorah, is not itself a religious symbol. Although Christmas trees once carried religious connotations, today they typify the secular celebration of Christmas. Numerous Americans place Christmas trees in their homes without subscribing to Christian religious beliefs, and when the city's tree stands alone in front of the City-County Building, it is not considered an endorsement of Christian faith. Indeed, a 40-foot Christmas tree was one of the objects that validated the creche in *Lynch*. The widely accepted view of the Christmas tree as the preeminent secular symbol of the Christmas holiday season serves to emphasize the secular component of the message communicated by other elements of an accompanying holiday display, including the Chanukah menorah.

The tree, moreover, is clearly the predominant element in the city's display. The 45-foot tree occupies the central position beneath the middle archway in front of the Grant Street entrance to the City-County Building; the 18-foot menorah is positioned to one side. Given this configuration, it is much more sensible to interpret the meaning of the menorah in light of the tree, rather than vice versa. In the shadow of the tree, the menorah is readily understood as simply a recognition that Christmas is not the only traditional way of observing the winter-holiday season. In these circumstances, then, the combination of the tree and the menorah communicates, not a simultaneous endorsement of both Christian and Jewish faith, but instead, a secular celebration of Christmas coupled with an acknowledgment of Chanukah as a contemporaneous alternative tradition.

Although the city has used a symbol with religious meaning as its representation of Chanukah, this is not a case in which the city has reasonable alternatives that are less religious in nature. It is difficult to imagine a predominantly secular symbol of Chanukah that the city could place next to its Christmas tree. An 18-foot dreidel would look out of place, and might be interpreted by some as mocking the celebration of Chanukah. The absence of a more secular alternative symbol is itself part of the context in which the city's actions must be judged in determining the likely effect of its use of the menorah. Where the government's secular message can be conveyed by two symbols, only one of which carries religious meaning, an observer reasonably might infer from the fact that the government has chosen to use the religious symbol that the government means to promote religious faith. But where, as here, no such choice has been made, this inference of endorsement is not present.

The Mayor's sign further diminishes the possibility that the tree and the menorah will be interpreted as a dual endorsement of Christianity and Judaism. The sign states that during the holiday season the city salutes liberty. Moreover, the sign draws upon the theme of light, common to both Chanukah and Christmas as winter festivals, and links that theme with this Nation's legacy of freedom, which allows an American to celebrate the holiday season in whatever way he wishes, religiously or otherwise. While no sign can disclaim an overwhelming message of endorsement, an "explanatory plaque" may confirm that in particular contexts the government's association with a religious symbol does not represent the government's sponsorship of religious beliefs. Here, the Mayor's sign serves to confirm what the context already reveals: that the display of the menorah is not an endorsement of religious faith but simply a recognition of cultural diversity.

Given all these considerations, it is not "sufficiently likely" that residents of Pittsburgh will perceive the combined display of the tree, the sign, and the menorah as an "endorsement" of "disapproval . . . of their individual religious choices." While an adjudication [a final determination] of the display's effect must take into account the perspective of one who is neither Christian nor Jewish, as well as of those who adhere to either of these religions, the constitutionality of its effect must also be judged according to the standard of a "reasonable observer." When measured against this standard, the menorah need not be excluded from this particular display. The Christmas tree alone in the Pittsburgh location does not endorse Christian belief; and . . . the addition of the menorah "cannot fairly be understood to" result in the simultaneous endorsement of Christian and Jewish faiths. On the contrary, for purposes of the Establishment Clause, the city's overall display must be understood as conveying the city's secular recognition of different traditions for celebrating the winter-holiday season.

The conclusion here that, in this particular context, the menorah's display does not have an effect of endorsing religious faith does not foreclose the possibility that the display of the menorah might violate either the "purpose" or "entanglement" prong of the *Lemon* analysis. These issues were not addressed by the Court of Appeals and may be considered by that court on remand [return to the lower court].

Lynch v. Donnelly confirms . . . the longstanding constitutional principle that government may not engage in a practice that has the effect of promoting or endorsing religious beliefs. The display of the creche in the County Courthouse has this unconstitutional effect. The display of the menorah in front of the City-County Building, however, does not have this effect, given its "particular physical setting."

The judgment of the Court of Appeals is affirmed [upheld] in part and reversed in part, and the cases are [returned] for further proceedings.

It is so ordered.

THE U.S. CONSTITUTION

THE U.S. CONSTITUTION

PREAMBLE

We the people of the United States, in order to form a more perfect union, establish justice, insure domestic tranquility, provide for the common defense, promote the general welfare, and secure the blessings of liberty to ourselves and our posterity, do ordain and establish this Constitution for the United States of America.

ARTICLE I

Section 1. All legislative powers herein granted shall be vested in a Congress of the United States, which shall consist of a Senate and House of Representatives.

Section 2. (1) The House of Representatives shall be composed of members chosen every second year by the people of the several states, and the electors in each state shall have the qualifications requisite for electors of the most numerous branch of the State Legislature.

(2) No person shall be a Representative who shall not have attained to the age of twenty-five years, and been seven years a citizen of the United States, and who shall not, when elected, be an inhabitant of that state in which he shall be chosen.

(3) Representatives and direct taxes shall be apportioned among the several states which may be included within this union, according to their respective numbers, which shall be determined by adding to the whole number of free persons, including those bound to service for a term of years, and excluding Indians not taxed, three-fifths of all other persons. The actual enumeration shall be made

within three years after the first meeting of the Congress of the United States, and within every subsequent term of ten years, in such manner as they shall by law direct. The number of Representatives shall not exceed one for every thirty thousand, but each state shall have at least one Representative; and until such enumeration shall be made, the State of New Hampshire shall be entitled to choose three, Massachusetts eight, Rhode Island and Providence Plantations one, Connecticut five, New York six, New Jersey four, Pennsylvania eight, Delaware one, Maryland six, Virginia ten, North Carolina five, South Carolina five, and Georgia three.

(4) When vacancies happen in the representation from any state, the executive authority thereof shall issue writs of election to fill such vacancies.

(5) The House of Representatives shall choose their Speaker and other Officers; and shall have the sole power of impeachment.

Section 3. (1) The Senate of the United States shall be composed of two Senators from each state, chosen by the legislature thereof, for six years; and each Senator shall have one vote.

(2) Immediately after they shall be assembled in consequence of the first election, they shall be divided as equally as may be into three classes. The seats of the Senators of the first class shall be vacated at the expiration of the second year, of the second class at the expiration of the fourth year, and of the third class at the expiration of the sixth year, so that one-third may be chosen every second year; and if vacancies happen by resignation, or otherwise, during the recess of the legislature of any state, the execu-

tive thereof may make temporary appointments until the next meeting of the legislature, which shall then fill such vacancies.

(3) No person shall be a Senator who shall not have attained to the age of thirty years, and been nine years a citizen of the United States, and who shall not, when elected, be an inhabitant of that state for which he shall be chosen.

(4) The Vice President of the United States shall be President of the Senate, but shall have no vote, unless they be equally divided.

(5) The Senate shall choose their other Officers, and also a President pro tempore, in the absence of the Vice President, or when he shall exercise the Office of President of the United States.

(6) The Senate shall have the sole power to try all impeachments. When sitting for that purpose, they shall be on oath or affirmation. When the President of the United States is tried, the Chief Justice shall preside: and no person shall be convicted without the concurrence of two-thirds of the members present.

(7) Judgment in cases of impeachment shall not extend further than to removal from office, and disqualification to hold and enjoy any office of honor, trust, or profit under the United States: but the party convicted shall nevertheless be liable and subject to indictment, trial, judgment, and punishment, according to law.

Section 4. (1) The times, places and manner of holding elections for Senators and Representatives, shall be prescribed in each state by the legislature thereof; but the Congress may at any time by law make or alter such regulations, except as to the places of choosing Senators.

(2) The Congress shall assemble at least once in every year, and such meeting shall be on the first Monday in December, unless they shall by law appoint a different day.

Section 5. (1) Each House shall be the judge of the elections, returns, and qualifications of its own members, and a majority of each shall constitute a quorum to do business; but a smaller number may adjourn from day to day, and may be authorized to compel the attendance of absent members, in such manner, and under such penalties as each House may provide.

(2) Each House may determine the rules of its proceedings, punish its members for disorderly behavior, and, with the concurrence of two-thirds, expel a member.

(3) Each House shall keep a journal of its proceedings, and from time to time publish the same, excepting such parts as may in their judgment require secrecy; and the yeas and nays of the members of either House on any question shall, at the desire of one-fifth of those present, be entered on the journal.

(4) Neither House, during the Session of Congress, shall, without the consent of the other, adjourn for more than three days, nor to any other place than that in which the two Houses shall be sitting.

Section 6. (1) The Senators and Representatives shall receive a compensation for their services, to be ascertained
by law, and paid out of the Treasury of the United States.
They shall in all cases, except treason, felony and breach
of the peace, be privileged from arrest during their attendance at the session of their respective Houses, and in
going to and returning from the same; and for any speech
or debate in either House, they shall not be questioned in
any other place.

(2) No Senator or Representative shall, during the time
for which he was elected, be appointed to any civil office
under the authority of the United States, which shall have
been created, or the emoluments whereof shall have been
increased during such time and no person holding any office under the United States, shall be a member of either
House during his continuance in office.

Section 7. (1) All bills for raising revenue shall originate
in the House of Representatives; but the Senate may propose or concur with amendments as on other bills.

(2) Every bill which shall have passed the House of Representatives and the Senate, shall, before it become a law,
be presented to the President of the United States; if he
approve he shall sign it, but if not he shall return it, with
his objections to the House in which it shall have originated, who shall enter the objections at large on their journal,
and proceed to reconsider it. If after such reconsideration
two-thirds of that House shall agree to pass the bill, it
shall be sent together with the objections, to the other
House, by which it shall likewise be reconsidered, and if
approved by two-thirds of that House, it shall become a
law. But in all such cases the votes of both Houses shall
be determined by yeas and nays, and the names of the per-

sons voting for and against the bill shall be entered on the
journal of each House respectively. If any bill shall not
be returned by the President within ten days (Sundays excepted) after it shall have been presented to him, the same
shall be a law, in like manner as if he had signed it, unless
the Congress by their adjournment prevent its return in
which case it shall not be a law.

(3) Every order, resolution, or vote, to which the concurrence of the Senate and House of Representatives may be
necessary (except on a question of adjournment) shall be
presented to the President of the United States; and before the same shall take effect, shall be approved by him,
or being disapproved by him, shall be repassed by two-
thirds of the Senate and House of Representatives, according to the rules and limitations prescribed in the case of a
bill.

Section 8. (1) The Congress shall have the power to lay
and collect taxes, duties, imposts and excises, to pay the
debts and provide for the common defense and general
welfare of the United States; but all duties, imposts and
excises shall be uniform throughout the United States;

(2) To borrow money on the credit of the United States;

(3) To regulate commerce with foreign nations, and
among the several states, and with the Indian Tribes;

(4) To establish an uniform Rule of Naturalization, and
uniform laws on the subject of bankruptcies throughout
the United States;

(5) To coin money, regulate the value thereof, and of foreign coin, and fix the standard of weights and measures;

(6) To provide for the punishment of counterfeiting the securities and current coin of the United States;

(7) To establish Post Offices and Post Roads;

(8) To promote the progress of science and useful arts, by securing for limited times to authors and inventors the exclusive right to their respective writings and discoveries;

(9) To constitute tribunals inferior to the Supreme Court;

(10) To define and punish piracies and felonies committed on the high seas, and offenses against the Law of Nations;

(11) To declare war, grant Letters of marque and reprisal, and make rules concerning captures on land and water;

(12) To raise and support armies, but no appropriation of money to that use shall be for a longer term than two years;

(13) To provide and maintain a Navy;

(14) To make rules for the government and regulation of the land and naval forces;

(15) To provide for calling forth the Militia to execute the laws of the Union, suppress insurrections and repel invasions;

(16) To provide for organizing, arming, and disciplining, the Militia, and for governing such part of them as may be employed in the service of the United States, reserving to the states respectively, the appointment of the Officers,

and the authority of training the Militia according to the discipline prescribed by Congress;

(17) To exercise exclusive legislation in all cases whatsoever, over such district (not exceeding ten miles square) as may, by cession of particular states, and the acceptance of Congress, become the Seat of the Government of the United States, and to exercise like authority over all places purchased by the consent of the legislature of the state in which the same shall be, for the erection of forts, magazines, arsenals, dockyards, and other needful buildings; - and

(18) To make all laws which shall be necessary and proper for carrying into execution the foregoing powers, and all other powers vested by this Constitution in the Government of the United States, or in any Department or Officer thereof.

Section 9. (1) The migration or importation of such persons as any of the states now existing shall think proper to admit, shall not be prohibited by the Congress prior to the year one thousand eight hundred and eight, but a tax or duty may be imposed on such importation, not exceeding ten dollars for each person.

(2) The privilege of the writ of habeas corpus shall not be suspended, unless when in cases of rebellion or invasion the public safety may require it.

(3) No bill of attainder or ex post facto law shall be passed.

(4) No capitation, or other direct, tax shall be laid, unless in proportion to the census or enumeration herein before directed to be taken.

(5) No tax or duty shall be laid on articles exported from any state.

(6) No preference shall be given by any regulation of commerce or revenue to the ports of one state over those of another: nor shall vessels bound to, or from, one state be obliged to enter, clear, or pay duties in another.

(7) No money shall be drawn from the Treasury, but in consequence of appropriations made by law; and a regular statement and account of the receipts and expenditures of all public money shall be published from time to time.

(8) No title of nobility shall be granted by the United States: and no person holding any office of profit or trust under them, shall, without the consent of the Congress, accept of any present, emolument, office, or title, of any kind whatever, from any King, Prince, or foreign State.

Section 10. (1) No state shall enter into any treaty, alliance, or confederation; grant letters of marque and reprisal; coin money; emit bills of credit; make any thing but gold and silver coin a tender in payment of debts; pass any bill of attainder, ex post facto law, or law impairing the obligation of contracts, or grant any title of nobility.

(2) No state shall, without the consent of the Congress, lay any imposts or duties on imports or exports, except what may be absolutely necessary for executing its inspection laws: and the net produce of all duties and imposts, laid by any state on imports or exports, shall be for the use of

the Treasury of the United States; and all such laws shall be subject to the revision and control of the Congress.

(3) No state shall, without the consent of Congress, lay any duty of tonnage, keep troops, or ships of war in time of peace, enter into any agreement or compact with another state, or with a foreign power, or engage in war, unless actually invaded, or in such imminent danger as will not admit of delay.

ARTICLE II

Section 1. (1) The executive power shall be vested in a President of the United States of America. He shall hold his office during the term of four years, and, together with the Vice President, chosen for the same term, be elected, as follows:

(2) Each state shall appoint, in such manner as the legislature thereof may direct, a number of electors, equal to the whole number of Senators and Representatives to which the state may be entitled in the Congress; but no Senator or Representative, or person holding an office of trust or profit under the United States, shall be appointed an Elector.

(3) The electors shall meet in their respective states, and vote by ballot for two persons, of whom one at least shall not be an inhabitant of the same state with themselves. And they shall make a list of all the persons voted for, and of the number of votes for each; which list they shall sign and certify, and transmit sealed to the Seat of the Government of the United States, directed to the President of the Senate. The President of the Senate shall, in the presence of the Senate and House of Representatives,

open all the certificates, and the votes shall then be counted. The person having the greatest number of votes shall be the President, if such number be a majority of the whole number of electors appointed; and if there be more than one who have such majority, and have an equal number of votes, then the House of Representatives shall immediately choose by ballot one of them for President; and if no person have a majority, then from the five highest on the list the said House shall in like manner choose the President. But in choosing the President, the votes shall be taken by states the representation from each state having one vote; a quorum for this purpose shall consist of a member or members from two-thirds of the states, and a majority of all the states shall be necessary to a choice. In every case, after the choice of the President, the person having the greater number of votes of the electors shall be the Vice President. But if there should remain two or more who have equal votes, the Senate shall choose from them by ballot the Vice President.

(4) The Congress may determine the time of choosing the Electors, and the day on which they shall give their votes; which day shall be the same throughout the United States.

(5) No person except a natural born citizen, or a citizen of the United States, at the time of the adoption of this Constitution, shall be eligible to the Office of President; neither shall any person be eligible to that Office who shall not have attained to the age of thirty-five years, and been fourteen years a resident within the United States.

(6) In case of the removal of the President from Office, or of his death, resignation or inability to discharge the powers and duties of the said Office, the same shall devolve on the Vice President, and the Congress may by law

provide for the case of removal, death, resignation or inability, both of the President and Vice President, declaring
what Officer shall then act as President, and such Officer
shall act accordingly, until the disability be removed, or a
President shall be elected.

(7) The President shall, at stated times, receive for his
services, a compensation, which shall neither be increased
nor diminished during the period for which he shall have
been elected, and he shall not receive within that period
any other emolument from the United States, or any of
them.

(8) Before he enter on the execution of his office, he shall
take the following oath or affirmation: "I do solemnly
swear (or affirm) that I will faithfully execute the Office
of President of the United States, and will to the best of
my ability, preserve, protect and defend the Constitution
of the United States."

Section 2. (1) The President shall be Commander in Chief
of the Army and Navy of the United States, and of the
militia of the several states, when called into the actual
service of the United States; he may require the opinion,
in writing, of the principal Officer in each of the Executive Departments, upon any subject relating to the duties
of their respective Offices, and he shall have power to
grant reprieves and pardons for offenses against the United States, except in cases of impeachment.

(2) He shall have power, by and with the advice and consent of the Senate to make treaties, provided two-thirds of
the Senators present concur; and he shall nominate, and
by and with the advice and consent of the Senate, shall appoint Ambassadors, other public Ministers and Consuls,

Judges of the supreme Court, and all other Officers of the United States, whose appointments are not herein otherwise provided for, and which shall be established by law; but the Congress may by law vest the appointment of such inferior Officers, as they think proper, in the President alone, in the courts of law, or in the heads of departments.

(3) The President shall have power to fill up all vacancies that may happen during the recess of the Senate, by granting commissions which shall expire at the end of their next session.

Section 3. He shall from time to time give to the Congress information of the State of the Union, and recommend to their consideration such measures as he shall judge necessary and expedient; he may, on extraordinary occasions, convene both Houses, or either of them, and in case of disagreement between them, with respect to the time of adjournment, he may adjourn them to such time as he shall think proper; he shall receive Ambassadors and other public Ministers; he shall take care that the laws be faithfully executed, and shall commission all the Officers of the United States.

Section 4. The President, Vice President and all civil Officers of the United States, shall be removed from office on impeachment for, and conviction of, treason, bribery, or other high crimes and misdemeanors.

ARTICLE III

Section 1. The judicial power of the United States, shall be vested in one supreme Court, and in such inferior courts as the Congress may from time to time ordain and establish. The Judges, both of the supreme and inferior courts, shall hold their Offices during good behaviour, and shall, at stated times, receive for their services a compensation, which shall not be diminished during their continuance in office.

Section 2. (1) The judicial power shall extend to all cases, in law and equity, arising under this Constitution, the laws of the United States, and treaties made, or which shall be made, under their authority; - to all cases affecting Ambassadors, other public Ministers and Consuls; - to all cases of admiralty and maritime jurisdiction; - to controversies to which the United States shall be a party; - to controversies between two or more states; - between a state and citizens of another state; - between citizens of different states; - between citizens of the same state claiming lands under the grants of different states, and between a state, or the citizens thereof, and foreign states, citizens or subjects.

(2) In all cases affecting Ambassadors, other public Ministers and Consuls, and those in which a state shall be a party, the supreme Court shall have original jurisdiction. In all the other cases before mentioned, the supreme Court shall have appellate jurisdiction, both as to law and fact, with such exceptions, and under such regulations as the Congress shall make.

(3) The trial of all crimes, except in cases of impeachment, shall be by jury; and such trial shall be held in the state where the said crimes shall have been committed; but when not committed within any state, the trial shall be at such place or places as the Congress may by law have directed.

Section 3. (1) Treason against the United States, shall consist only in levying war against them, or, in adhering to their enemies, giving them aid and comfort. No person shall be convicted of treason unless on the testimony of two witnesses to the same overt act, or on confession in open Court.

(2) The Congress shall have power to declare the punishment of treason, but no Attainder of Treason shall work corruption of blood, or forfeiture except during the life of the person attainted.

ARTICLE IV

Section 1. Full faith and credit shall be given in each state to the public acts, records, and judicial proceedings of every other state. And the Congress may by general laws prescribe the manner in which such acts, records and proceedings shall be proved, and the effect thereof.

Section 2. (1) The citizens of each state shall be entitled to all privileges and immunities of citizens in the several states.

(2) A person charged in any state with treason, felony, or other crime, who shall flee from justice, and be found in another state, shall on demand of the executive authority of the state from which he fled, be delivered up, to be removed to the state having jurisdiction of the crime.

(3) No person held to service or labor in one state, under the laws thereof, escaping into another, shall, in consequence of any law or regulation therein, be discharged from such service or labor, but shall be delivered up on

claim of the party to whom such service or labor may be due.

Section 3. (1) New states may be admitted by the Congress into this union; but no new state shall be formed or erected within the jurisdiction of any other state; nor any state be formed by the junction of two or more states, or parts of states, without the consent of the legislatures of the states concerned as well as of the Congress.

(2) The Congress shall have power to dispose of and make all needful rules and regulations respecting the territory or other property belonging to the United States; and nothing in this Constitution shall be so construed as to prejudice any claims of the United States, or of any particular state.

Section 4. The United States shall guarantee to every state in this union a Republican form of government, and shall protect each of them against invasion; and on application of the legislature, or of the executive (when the legislature cannot be convened) against domestic violence.

ARTICLE V

The Congress, whenever two-thirds of both Houses shall deem it necessary, shall propose amendments to this Constitution, or, on the application of the legislatures of two-thirds of the several states, shall call a convention for proposing amendments, which, in either case, shall be valid to all intents and purposes, as part of this constitution, when ratified by the legislatures of three-fourths of the several states, or by conventions in three-fourths thereof, as the one or the other mode of ratification may be proposed by the Congress; provided that no amendment which may be made prior to the year one thousand eight hundred and eight shall in any manner affect the first and fourth clauses in the Ninth Section of the first Article; and that no state, without its consent, shall be deprived of its equal suffrage in the Senate.

ARTICLE VI

(1) All debts contracted and engagements entered into, before the adoption of this Constitution shall be as valid against the United States under this Constitution, as under the Confederation.

(2) This Constitution, and the laws of the United States which shall be made in pursuance thereof; and all treaties made, or which shall be made, under the authority of the United States, shall be the supreme law of the land; and the Judges in every state shall be bound thereby, any thing in the Constitution or laws of any state to the contrary notwithstanding.

(3) The Senators and Representatives before mentioned, and the Members of the several State Legislatures, and all executive and judicial Officers, both of the United States and of the several states, shall be bound by oath or affirmation, to support this Constitution; but no religious test shall ever be required as a qualification to any office or public trust under the United States.

ARTICLE VII

The ratification of the Conventions of nine states shall be sufficient for the establishment of this Constitution between the states so ratifying the same.

AMENDMENT I (1791)

Congress shall make no law respecting an establishment of religion, or prohibiting the free exercise thereof; or abridging the freedom of speech, or of the press; or the right of the people peaceably to assemble, and to petition the Government for a redress of grievances.

AMENDMENT II (1791)

A well regulated Militia, being necessary to the security of a free state, the right of the people to keep and bear arms, shall not be infringed.

AMENDMENT III (1791)

No soldier shall, in time of peace be quartered in any house, without the consent of the owner, nor in time of war, but in a manner to be prescribed by law.

AMENDMENT IV (1791)

The right of the people to be secure in their persons, houses, papers, and effects, against unreasonable searches and seizures, shall not be violated, and no warrants shall issue, but upon probable cause, supported by oath or affirmation, and particularly describing the place to be searched, and the persons or things to be seized.

AMENDMENT V (1791)

No person shall be held to answer for a capital, or otherwise infamous crime, unless on a presentment or indictment of a Grand Jury, except in cases arising in the land or naval forces, or in the Militia, when in actual service in time of war or public danger; nor shall any person be subject for the same offense to be twice put in jeopardy of life or limb; nor shall be compelled in any criminal case to be a witness against himself, nor be deprived of life, liberty, or property, without due process of law; nor shall private property be taken for public use, without just compensation.

AMENDMENT VI (1791)

In all criminal prosecutions, the accused shall enjoy the right to a speedy and public trial, by an impartial jury of the state and district wherein the crime shall have been committed, which district shall have been previously ascertained by law, and to be informed of the nature and cause of the accusation; to be confronted with the witnesses against him; to have compulsory process for obtaining witnesses in his favor, and to have the assistance of counsel for his defense.

AMENDMENT VII (1791)

In suits at common law, where the value in controversy shall exceed twenty dollars, the right of trial by jury shall be preserved, and no fact tried by jury, shall be otherwise re-examined in any court of the United States, than according to the rules of the common law.

AMENDMENT VIII (1791)

Excessive bail shall not be required, nor excessive fines imposed, nor cruel and unusual punishments inflicted.

AMENDMENT IX (1791)

The enumeration in the Constitution, of certain rights,
shall not be construed to deny or disparage others retained
by the people.

AMENDMENT X (1791)

The powers not delegated to the United States by the Constitution, nor prohibited by it to the States, are reserved to
the States respectively, or to the people.

AMENDMENT XI (1798)

The judicial power of the United States shall not be construed to extend to any suit in law or equity, commenced
or prosecuted against one of the United States by citizens
of another state, or by citizens or subjects of any foreign
state.

AMENDMENT XII (1804)

The Electors shall meet in their respective states and vote
by ballot for President and Vice-President, one of whom,
at least, shall not be an inhabitant of the same state with
themselves; they shall name in their ballots the person
voted for as President, and in distinct ballots the person
voted for as Vice-President, and they shall make distinct
lists of all persons voted for as President, and of all persons voted for as Vice-President, and of the number of
votes for each, which lists they shall sign and certify, and
transmit sealed to the seat of the government of the United States, directed to the President of the Senate; - the
President of the Senate shall, in the presence of the Senate
and House of Representatives, open all the certificates and

the votes shall then be counted; - the person having the
greatest number of votes for President, shall be the President, if such number be a majority of the whole number
of electors appointed; and if no person have such majority, then from the persons having the highest numbers not
exceeding three on the list of those voted for as President,
the House of Representatives shall choose immediately, by
ballot, the President. But in choosing the President, the
votes shall be taken by states, the representation from
each state having one vote; a quorum for this purpose
shall consist of a member or members from two-thirds of
the states, and a majority of all the states shall be necessary to a choice. And if the House of Representatives
shall not choose a President whenever the right of choice
shall devolve upon them before the fourth day of March
next following, then the Vice-President shall act as President, as in the case of the death or other constitutional
disability of the President. - The person having the greatest number of votes as Vice-President, shall be the Vice-
President, if such number be a majority of the whole
number of Electors appointed, and if no person have a
majority, then from the two highest numbers on the list,
the Senate shall choose the Vice-President; a quorum for
the purpose shall consist of two-thirds of the whole number of Senators, and a majority of the whole number shall
be necessary to a choice. But no person constitutionally
ineligible to the office of President shall be eligible to
that of Vice-President of the United States.

AMENDMENT XIII (1865)

Section 1. Neither slavery nor involuntary servitude, except as a punishment for crime whereof the party shall
have been duly convicted, shall exist within the United
States, or any place subject to their jurisdiction.

Section 2. Congress shall have power to enforce this article by appropriate legislation.

AMENDMENT XIV (1868)

Section 1. All persons born or naturalized in the United States, and subject to the jurisdiction thereof, are citizens of the United States and of the state wherein they reside. No state shall make or enforce any law which shall abridge the privileges or immunities of citizens of the United States; nor shall any state deprive any person of life, liberty, or property, without due process of law; nor deny to any person within its jurisdiction the equal protection of the laws.

Section 2. Representatives shall be apportioned among the several states according to their respective numbers, counting the whole number of persons in each State excluding Indians not taxed. But when the right to vote at any election for the choice of electors for President and Vice President of the United States, Representatives in Congress, the Executive and Judicial officers of a state, or the members of the Legislature thereof, is denied to any of the male inhabitants of such state, being twenty-one years of age, and citizens of the United States, or in any way abridged, except for participation in rebellion, or other crime, the basis of representation therein shall be reduced in the proportion which the number of such male citizens shall bear to the whole number of male citizens twenty-one years of age in such state.

Section 3. No person shall be a Senator or Representative in Congress, or elector of President and Vice President, or hold any office, civil or military, under the United States, or under any state, who having previously taken an oath, as a member of Congress, or as an officer of the United States, or as a member of any state legislature, or as an executive or judicial officer of any state, to support the Constitution of the United States, shall have engaged in insurrection or rebellion against the same, or given aid or comfort to the enemies thereof. But Congress may by a vote of two-thirds of each House, remove such disability.

Section 4. The validity of the public debt of the United States, authorized by law, including debts incurred for payment of pensions and bounties for services in suppressing insurrection or rebellion, shall not be questioned. But neither the United States nor any state shall assume or pay any debt or obligation incurred in aid of insurrection or rebellion against the United States, or any claim for the loss or emancipation of any slave; but all such debts, obligations and claims shall be held illegal and void.

Section 5. The Congress shall have power to enforce, by appropriate legislation, the provisions of this article.

AMENDMENT XV (1870)

Section 1. The right of citizens of the United States to vote shall not be denied or abridged by the United States or by any state on account of race, color, or previous condition of servitude.

Section 2. The Congress shall have power to enforce this article by appropriate legislation.

AMENDMENT XVI (1913)

The Congress shall have power to lay and collect taxes on incomes, from whatever source derived, without apportionment among the several states, and without regard to any census or enumeration.

AMENDMENT XVII (1913)

(1) The Senate of the United States shall be composed of two Senators from each state, elected by the people thereof, for six years; and each Senator shall have one vote. The electors in each State shall have the qualifications requisite for electors of the most numerous branch of the state legislatures.

(2) When vacancies happen in the representation of any state in the Senate, the executive authority of such state shall issue writs of election to fill such vacancies: *provided*, that the legislature of any state may empower the executive thereof to make temporary appointments until the people fill the vacancies by election as the legislature may direct.

(3) This amendment shall not be so construed as to affect the election or term of any Senator chosen before it becomes valid as part of the Constitution.

AMENDMENT XVIII (1919)

Section 1. After one year from the ratification of this article the manufacture, sale, or transportation of intoxicating liquors within, the importation thereof into, or the exportation thereof from the United States and all territory subject to the jurisdiction thereof for beverage purposes is hereby prohibited.

Section 2. The Congress and the several states shall have concurrent power to enforce this article by appropriate legislation.

Section 3. This article shall be inoperative unless it shall have been ratified as an amendment to the Constitution by the legislatures of the several states, as provided in the Constitution, within seven years from the date of the submission hereof to the states by the Congress.

AMENDMENT XIX (1920)

(1) The right of citizens of the United States to vote shall not be denied or abridged by the United States or by any state on account of sex.

(2) Congress shall have power to enforce this article by appropriate legislation.

AMENDMENT XX (1933)

Section 1. The terms of the President and Vice President shall end at noon on the 20th day of January, and the terms of Senators and Representatives at noon on the 3d day of January, of the years in which such terms would have ended if this article had not been ratified; and the terms of their successors shall then begin.

Section 2. The Congress shall assemble at least once in every year, and such meeting shall begin at noon on the 3d day of January, unless they shall by law appoint a different day.

Section 3. If, at the time fixed for the beginning of the term of the President, the President elect shall have died, the Vice President elect shall become President. If the President shall not have been chosen before the time fixed for the beginning of his term, or if the President elect shall have failed to qualify, then the Vice President elect shall act as President until a President shall have qualified; and the Congress may by law provide for the case wherein neither a President elect nor a Vice President elect shall have qualified, declaring who shall then act as President, or the manner in which one who is to act shall be selected, and such person shall act accordingly until a President or Vice President shall have qualified.

Section 4. The Congress may by law provide for the case of the death of any of the persons from whom the House of Representatives may choose a President whenever the right of choice shall have devolved upon them, and for the case of the death of any of the persons from whom the Senate may choose a Vice President whenever the right of choice shall have devolved upon them.

Section 5. Sections 1 and 2 shall take effect on the 15th day of October following the ratification of this article.

Section 6. This article shall be inoperative unless it shall have been ratified as an amendment to the Constitution by the legislatures of three-fourths of the several states within seven years from the date of its submission.

AMENDMENT XXI (1933)

Section 1. The eighteenth article of amendment to the Constitution of the United States is hereby repealed.

Section 2. The transportation or importation into any state, territory, or possession of the United States for delivery or use therein of intoxicating liquors, in violation of the laws thereof, is hereby prohibited.

Section 3. This article shall be inoperative unless it shall have been ratified as an amendment to the Constitution by conventions in the several states, as provided in the Constitution, within seven years from the date of the submission hereof to the states by the Congress.

AMENDMENT XXII (1951)

Section 1. No person shall be elected to the office of the President more than twice, and no person who has held the office of President, or acted as President, for more than two years of a term to which some other person was elected President shall be elected to the office of President more than once. But this Article shall not apply to any person holding the office of President when this Article was proposed by the Congress, and shall not prevent any person who may be holding the office of President, or acting as President, during the term within which this Article becomes operative from holding the office of President or acting as President during the remainder of such term.

Section 2. This article shall be inoperative unless it shall have been ratified as an amendment to the Constitution by the legislatures of three-fourths of the several states within seven years from the date of its submission to the states by the Congress.

AMENDMENT XXIII (1961)

Section 1. The District constituting the seat of Government of the United States shall appoint in such manner as the Congress may direct:

A number of electors of President and Vice President equal to the whole number of Senators and Representatives in Congress to which the District would be entitled if it were a state, but in no event more than the least populous state; they shall be in addition to those appointed by the states, but they shall be considered, for the purposes of the election of President and Vice President, to be electors appointed by a state; and they shall meet in the District and perform such duties as provided by the twelfth article of amendment.

Section 2. The Congress shall have power to enforce this article by appropriate legislation.

AMENDMENT XXIV (1964)

Section 1. The right of citizens of the United States to vote in any primary or other election for President or Vice President, for electors for President or Vice President, or for Senator or Representative in Congress, shall not be denied or abridged by the United States, or any state by reason of failure to pay any poll tax or other tax.

Section 2. The Congress shall have power to enforce this article by appropriate legislation.

AMENDMENT XXV (1967)

Section 1. In case of the removal of the President from office or of his death or resignation, the Vice President shall become President.

Section 2. Whenever there is a vacancy in the office of the Vice President, the President shall nominate a Vice President who shall take office upon confirmation by a majority vote of both Houses of Congress.

Section 3. Whenever the President transmits to the President pro tempore of the Senate and the Speaker of the House of Representatives his written declaration that he is unable to discharge the powers and duties of his office, and until he transmits to them a written declaration to the contrary, such powers and duties shall be discharged by the Vice President as Acting President.

Section 4. Whenever the Vice President and a majority of either the principal officers of the executive departments or of such other body as Congress may by law provide, transmit to the President pro tempore of the Senate and the Speaker of the House of Representatives their written declaration that the President is unable to discharge the powers and duties of his office, the Vice President shall immediately assume the powers and duties of the office as Acting President.

Thereafter, when the President transmits to the President pro tempore of the Senate and the Speaker of the House of Representatives his written declaration that no inability exists, he shall resume the powers and duties of his office unless the Vice President and a majority of either the principal officers of the executive department or of such other body as Congress may by law provide, transmit within four days to the President pro tempore of the Senate and the Speaker of the House of Representatives their written declaration and the President is unable to discharge the powers and duties of his office. Thereupon Congress shall decide the issue, assembling within forty-eight hours for that purpose if not in session. If the Congress, within twenty-one days after receipt of the latter written declaration, or, if Congress is not in session, within twenty-one days after Congress is required to assemble, determines by two-thirds vote of both Houses that the President is unable to discharge the power and duties of his office, the Vice President shall continue to discharge the same as Acting President; otherwise, the President shall resume the powers and duties of his office.

AMENDMENT XXVI (1971)

Section 1. The right of citizens of the United States, who are eighteen years of age or older, to vote shall not be denied or abridged by the United States or by any state on account of age.

Section 2. The Congress shall have power to enforce this article by appropriate legislation.

BIBLIOGRAPHY

EXECUTIVE PRIVILEGE

Ball, Howard, *"We Have A Duty": The Supreme Court and the Watergate Tapes Litigation*, New York: Greenwood Press, 1990.

Bernstein, Carl, and Bob Woodward, *All The President's Men*, New York: Simon & Schuster, 1974.

Breckenridge, Adam Carlyle, *The Executive Privilege: Presidential Control Over Information*, Lincoln: University of Nebraska Press, 1974.

Clinton, Robert Lowry, *Marbury v. Madison and Judicial Review*, Lawrence: University Press of Kansas, 1989.

Dewey, Donald O., *Marshall vs. Jefferson: The Political Background of Madison v. Marbury*, New York: Knopf, 1970.

Friedman, Leon, *United States v. Nixon: The President Before the Supreme Court*, New York: Chelsea House Publishers, 1974.

CLEAR AND PRESENT DANGER

Anastopio, George, *Freedom of Speech and the First Amendment*, Detroit: University of Detroit Law Journal, 1964.

Baker, C. Edwin, *Human Liberty and Freedom of Speech*, New York: Oxford University Press, 1989.

Chafee, Zachariah, *Freedom of Speech*, New York: Harcourt, Brace & Howe, 1920.

Hentoff, Nat, *The First Freedom: A Tumultuous History of Free Speech in America*, New York: Delacorte Press, 1980.

Nelles, Walter, *Espionage Act Cases, With Certain Others on Related Points: New Law in Making as to Criminal Utterance in War-Time*, New York: National Civil Liberties Bureau, 1918.

FORCED STERILIZATION

Sloan, Irving J., *The Law Governing Abortion, Contraception, and Sterilization*, New York: Oceana Publications, 1988.

Macklin, Ruth, and Willard Gaylin, eds., *Mental Retardation and Sterilization: A Problem of Competency and Paternalism*, New York: Plenum Press, 1981.

Reilly, Phillip, *The Surgical Solution: A History of Involuntary Sterilization in the United States*, Baltimore: Johns Hopkins University Press, 1991.

MOB JUSTICE

Carter, Dan T., *Scottsboro: A Tragedy of the American South*, rev. ed., Baton Rouge: Louisiana State University Press, 1979.

Chalmers, Allan Knight, *They Shall Be Free*, Garden City: Doubleday, 1951.

Covin, Kelly, *Hear That Train Blow: A Novel About the Scottsboro Case*, New York: Delacorte Press, 1970.

Norris, Clarence, and Sybil D. Washington, *The Last of the Scottsboro Boys: An Autobiography*, New York: Putnam, 1979.

Patterson, Haywood, and Earl Conrad, *Scottsboro Boy*, Garden City: Doubleday, 1950.

PLEDGE OF ALLEGIANCE

Manwering, David Roger, *Render Unto Caesar: The Flag-Salute Controversy*, Chicago: University of Chicago Press, 1962.

Stevens, Leonard A., *Salute! The Case of the Bible vs. the Flag*, New York: Coward, McCann & Geoghegan, 1973.

Swanson, June, *I Pledge Allegiance*, Minneapolis: Carolrhoda Books, 1990.

ILLEGAL SEARCH AND SEIZURE

Stevens, Leonard, *Trespass! The People's Privacy vs. The Power of the Police*, New York: Coward, McCann & Geoghegan, 1977.

Waddington, Lawrence C., *Arrest, Search, and Seizure*, Beverly Hills: Glencoe Press, 1974.

INTERRACIAL MARRIAGE

Cretser, Gary A., and Joseph J. Leon, eds., *Intermarriage in the United States*, Binghamton: Haworth Press, 1982.

Huber, Patrick, *Two Races Beyond the Altar*, Boston: Branden Publishing Company, 1976.

MONKEY TRIALS

DeCamp, L. Sprague, *The Great Monkey Trail*, New York, Doubleday, 1968.

Larson, Edward J., *Trial and Error: The American Controversy Over Creation and Evolution*, New York: Oxford University Press, 1985.

McGowen, Tom, *The Great Monkey Trial: Science vs. Fundamentalism in America*, New York: Franklin Watts, 1990.

Scopes, John T., and James Presley, *Center of the Storm: Memoirs of John T. Scopes*, New York: Holt, Rinehart & Winston, 1967.

Zetterberg, J. Peter, *Evolution vs. Creationism*, Phoenix: The Oryx Press, 1983.

SEXUAL HARASSMENT

Backhouse, Constance, and Leah Cohen, *The Secret Oppression: Sexual Harassment of Working Women*, Toronto: MacMillan of Canada, 1978.

DeCrow, Karen, *Sexist Justice*, New York: Random House, 1974.

Farley, Lin, *Sexual Shakedown: The Sexual Harassment of Women on the Job*, New York: McGraw-Hill, 1978.

Neville, Kathleen, *Corporate Attractions: An Inside Account of Sexual Harassment with the New Sexual Rules for Men and Women on the Job*, Washington, DC: Acropolis Books, 1990.

CHURCH AND STATE

Alley, Robert S., *The Supreme Court on Church and State*, New York: Oxford University Press, 1988.

Kurland, Philip B., *Religion and the Law of Church and State and the Supreme Court*, Chicago: Aldine Publishing Company, 1962.

Miller, Robert Thomas, and Ronald B. Flowers, *Toward Benevolent Neutrality: Church, State, and the Supreme Court*, Waco: Baylor University Press, 1987.

THE SUPREME COURT

Agresto, John, *The Supreme Court and Constitutional Democracy*, Ithaca: Cornell University Press, 1984.

Cox, Archibald, *The Court and the Constitution*, New York: Houghton-Mifflin, 1988.

Dumbauld, Edward, *The Bill of Rights and What It Means Today*, New York: Greenwood Press, 1979.

Goode, Stephen, *The Controversial Court: Supreme Court Influences on American Life*, New York: Messner, 1982.

Lawson, Don, *Landmark Supreme Court Cases*, Hillside: Enslow Publishers, Inc., 1987.

Rehnquist, William H., *The Supreme Court: How It Was, How It Is*, New York: Morrow, 1987.

Woodward, Bob, and Scott Armstrong, *The Brethren: Inside the Supreme Court*, New York: Simon & Schuster, 1979.

Yudof, Mark, *When Government Speaks: Politics, Law, and Government Expression in America*, Berkeley and Los Angeles: University of California Press, 1983.

INDEX

Adams, John 14-15, 17
Allegheny County, Pennsylvania 170-173, 176-178, 185-187, 189-191, 194
American Bar Association 72
American Civil Liberties Union 70, 72, 170, 177
Anti-Evolution Act, Tennessee 138-142, 145, 148-149
Barnette, Walter 82, 84-85, 88
Bell, J.H. 48-49
Bible 70-71, 82, 84, 130, 134-135, 139-141, 148-149, 172, 185
Bill of Rights 72, 74, 78, 87, 90-92, 94, 102, 147, 178
Blackmun, Harry 170-171
Bryan, William Jennings 138
Buck, Carrie 48-49, 51
Burger, Warren 26-27
Capital case 59, 63-64, 67-68
Caroline County, Virginia 114-115
Censorship 87
Chabad 170, 176-178
Chanukah 170-171, 174-176, 178, 190-193
Checks and balances 30
Christmas 171-173, 176-177, 183, 186-193
Church and state, separation of 130-131, 133, 147-149, 170-171, 177-184, 186-189, 191-194
Civil liberty 16
Civil Rights Act of 1866 120
Civil Rights Act of 1964 152-153, 155-163, 166
Clark, Thomas 98-99, 133
Clear and present danger 44, 87
Cleveland, Ohio 98-99
Complaint procedure 152, 154-155, 163-166
Congress 14, 17, 20-21, 23, 29-30, 40-41, 44, 64, 91, 120-121, 144, 158, 165-166, 178
Conscription, see Draft

Also Available From Excellent Books

LANDMARK DECISIONS OF THE UNITED STATES SUPREME COURT II

SLAVERY

WOMEN'S SUFFRAGE

JAPANESE AMERICAN CONCENTRATION CAMPS

BIBLE READING IN THE PUBLIC SCHOOLS

THE BOOK BANNED IN BOSTON

RIGHTS OF THE ACCUSED

THE DEATH PENALTY

HOMOSEXUALITY

OFFENSIVE SPEECH

THE RIGHT TO DIE

MAUREEN HARRISON & STEVE GILBERT
EDITORS

ORDER FORM

(Please xerox this form so it will be available to other readers.)

Please send _____ copy(ies) of LANDMARK DECISIONS
_____ copy(ies) of LANDMARK DECISIONS II
_____ copy(ies) of LANDMARK DECISIONS III

OUR GUARANTEE: Any Excellent Book may be returned at any time for any reason and a full refund will be made.

Name: _____

Address: _____

City: _____ **State:** _____ **Zip:** _____

Price: $14.95 for LANDMARK DECISIONS
$15.95 for LANDMARK DECISIONS II
$15.95 for LANDMARK DECISIONS III
Shipping and handling included

Sales Tax: California residents add 7.25%

Mail your check or money order to: Excellent Books,
Post Office Box 7121, Beverly Hills, California 90212-7121